MISFITS

WINDING THE BALL

Alex Finlayson

PLAYS

MISFITS
WINDING THE BALL

First published in 1998 by Oberon Books Ltd.
(incorporating Absolute Classics),
521 Caledonian Road, London, N7 9RH.
Tel: 0171 607 3637 / Fax: 0171 607 3629

British Library Cataloguing-in-Publication Data
A catalogue record for this book is available from the British
Library.

ISBN: 1 870259 69 6

Cover design: Andrzej Klimowski

Typography: Richard Doust

Printed in Great Britain by Arrowhead Books Ltd., Reading.

CONTENTS

FOREWORD

New writers are the lifeblood of the theatre. All 'classics' were new plays once. Their excitement and enduring status arises from the genuinely contemporary, passionate and personal response playwrights had to the world they lived in.

Without new plays and new voices the theatre will rapidly become a place of nostalgia, complacency and emptiness. People will no longer feel that this live art form can compete with the many easier, more accessible and technologically proficient art forms of the next century.

Alex Finlayson is one of the most original and distinctive new writers I've come across. Her plays create vivid and authentic worlds underpinned by a fiercely personal moral vision. She deals with the most private sides of our lives but sees them in terms of the history and culture of her country. Her language is both direct and poetic, her stagecraft atmospheric and adventurous.

Winding the Ball takes place in one location in continuous time. When I first read it, it felt like *Flannery O'Connor* crossed with *Assault on Precinct 13*. The play felt contemporary in its rhythm, humour, economy and pressure but one was also aware of a far deeper resonance in this gallery of Americans trapped in a small town surrounded by unforgiving and brooding mountains. I loved the play because it was about love, death and the American way set amongst the rundown goods of a supermarket. A perfect fusion of setting and content.

Misfits is totally different. A massive piece in twenty scenes with a large cast about a public event. All the ingredients modern plays usually lack. Alex and I collaborated on *Misfits* for over three years so I can vouch for the accuracy of her research. All the famous figures who appear on stage were painstakingly examined. But ultimately *Misfits* is a play that looks at an extraordinary event in cinematic history that brought together some archetypal figures under the hot Nevada sun. The play shows the madness of the movies, the need for stars and myths and the troubled truth that lies underneath.

The nature and inevitable conflict between female and male creativity and imagination. Above all the play gives a voice to Marilyn Monroe, a figure endlessly fantasised and written about but often silenced by her devotees and enemies alike.

Both these plays were produced at the Royal Exchange Theatre to great critical and public acclaim. Alex is completing her next play for our theatre. I hope her work will be increasingly produced elsewhere (not least her own country). I know that both the people who work on her plays and the thousands that have seen them have laughed at her humour, been immersed in her world and felt a considerable power and depth from her creations. Welcome to a real playwright.

Greg Hersov
Manchester, March 1998

MISFITS

a filmic drama in twenty scenes

For Greg and Lisa

Who has twisted us around like this,
so that
no matter what we do, we are in the
posture
of someone going away?

Rilke

CHARACTERS

MARILYN

ARTHUR

JOHN

PAULA

CLARK

MONTY

ELI

FRANK

HARRY

THELMA

RALPH

WEATHERBY

BUZZY

PUSHY PHOTOGRAPHER

SKIP

PLUMBER

WHITEY

DOCTOR

WAITER

AGNES

KAY GABLE

NURSE

MAGNUM PHOTOGRAPHER

THE GIRL

THE LITTLE CHILD

REPORTERS (*Off.*)

Misfits was first performed at the Royal Exchange Theatre, Manchester on the 9th of May 1996 with the following cast:

MARILYN, Lisa Eichhorn
ARTHUR, Christian Burgess
JOHN, Stephen Yardley
PAULA, Paola Dionisotti
CLARK, Ray Lonnen
MONTY, James Clyde
ELI, Cliff Howells
FRANK, David Allister
HARRY, John Branwell
THELMA, Sandra Caron
RALPH/WEATHERBY, Claude Close
BUZZY/PUSHY PHOTOGRAPHER, John Axon
SKIP/ PLUMBER, Andrew Pope
WHITEY/DOCTOR/WAITER, Colin Meredith
AGNES/KAY GABLE/NURSE/
MAGNUM PHOTOGRAPHER, Maggie Tagney
THE GIRL, Emma Jay
THE LITTLE CHILD, Leona Read/Kimberley Heyes

DIRECTOR, Greg Hersov
ASSISTANT DIRECTOR, Marianne Elliott
SET DESIGNER, Laurie Dennett
COSTUME DESIGNER, David Short
LIGHTING DESIGNER, Johanna Town
SOUND DESIGNER, Scott Myers
DIALECT COACH, Julia Wilson Dickson
CHOREOGRAPHER, Sarah Taylor

Other parts played by members of the company.
The action takes place in 1960 over several months
of filming in Reno, Nevada.

ACT ONE

Scene 1

Night. Desert outside Reno. Car headlights violate the darkness and expose a woman. She is dressed casually in Capri pants and sandals. She wears no make-up and isn't particularly beautiful, just blonde. She is a MARILYN MONROE we've never seen before: a MARILYN off-screen, off-record. She revels in the desert, fairly dancing; her sandals wobble in the sand, but her footing is sure. PAULA STRASBERG enters from the offstage car. She is dressed in black with a black hat and a large black handbag. Her blackness makes her a figure in something portentous, like myth or allegory, but mostly there is something cartoonish about her and the way she inches out into the blinding light and desert night, wobbling in the sandy dirt, like an Italian peasant woman about to be executed in a comedy. MARILYN shines in the headlights, contrasting with the heavy darkness of PAULA.

MARILYN: Like a desert–

PAULA: It *is* the desert.

MARILYN: So quiet– Like being inside of nothing – (*To offstage.*) Rafe! Get out here this minute! You absolutely have to.

> (*The headlights go dark. In the moonlight, MARILYN glows incandescently, and PAULA is silhouetted like a distant mountain.*)

PAULA: Will you please watch out for snakes!

> (*MARILYN stoops in the sand. She picks up something, a twig or a rock. She hands it to PAULA, who drops it into her voluminous black handbag. RALPH ROBERTS enters from the offstage car. He is MARILYN's friend and masseur, a large bear of a man who also likes to barbecue.*)

MARILYN: (*To RALPH.*) Look!

PAULA: Believe me, we'll all have enough of the desert by the–

MARILYN: Shh! Don't talk!

> (*MARILYN revels in the silence, and we should feel it too. PAULA breaks the spell.*)

PAULA: I believe that the rationale for this drive was to put you to sleep.

MARILYN: Fuck sleep. This is what seduces her. This. Not a man– Not even– I found this! I mean– Be proud of me!

PAULA: I am always proud of you, dear, but we're all exhausted. I don't know what Arthur was thinking of–

(*MARILYN finds another treasure in the sand.*)

MARILYN: A little sea shell. From when it was the ocean–

(*MARILYN hands it to PAULA, who deposits it into the handbag.*)

PAULA: Dancing your heart out in that picture, then two weeks later they expect us here, ready to go.

MARILYN: I'm fine. Rafe's got my body, you've got my brain. Who's got my soul?

RALPH: You're on your own there, sweetie.

PAULA: No one's exempt from the human condition. Not even you. I'll be in the car.

(*PAULA exits to the car.*)

MARILYN: It's so quiet...

(*MARILYN is quiet for a minute. She takes in the desert. Then something comes to her.*)

"....infinite space
gnaws at our faces...."

(*The rest of it may not come as easily.*)

"....whom would it not remain for–
that longed-after
mildly disillusioning presence, which the solitary heart so painfully meets."

(*To RALPH.*) That's poetry, Rafe! But it's true. I think.

"Is it any less difficult for lovers?
But they keep on using each other to hide their own fate."
That's the rest of it.

PAULA: (*From offstage.*) Marilyn!

MARILYN: It all has to be wonderful, 'cause it's Arthur's picture, too. More even than mine. He makes a joke and

says I don't even have to be the blonde in this one!
(*Shift.*) When we get back, and I'm asleep, carry me.
Promise?

RALPH: Promise.

MARILYN: All the way up–

PAULA: (*Off.*) MARILYN!

MARILYN: I found this...

(*Lights fade.*)

Scene 2

(*Night. Harrah's casino bar. Reno. ELI WALLACH plays a slot machine. ARTHUR MILLER has a drink and an eye on the bar. He takes copious notes on a manuscript in front of him.*)

ELI: Come on, baby, come on, come on– (*Now to ARTHUR.*)
Hey, Miller– How about Guido? How about it's Guido
gets the girl?

(*ELI puts another coin in the slot machine.*)

Guido's our man.

ARTHUR: He needs her too much.

ELI: What? What's there to need? The man's got his own
damn airplane–

ARTHUR: She's had it with guys needing things from her.

ELI: So you give her to an old broken-down horse chaser–

ARTHUR: Every story has to be constructed with a spine,
Eli, a moral and theoretical strut which supports every
single action. It has to be sound–

ELI: So now we're making furniture–

ARTHUR: Inviolate. Like proof. The spine here is a man
who's willing to give. His personal freedom, his
celebration of life– that attraction the character of Gay
Langland has for all of us, not just her, is that he's a
symbol of a country where–

ELI: Symbol! We're making a picture here. And it ain't
French, Miller.

ARTHUR: A picture about love's capability to make things work– people work in a new way.

ELI: Listen, what we're talking about is old Clark Gable versus new young handsome robust Eli Wallach. Ask Marilyn.

ARTHUR: What?–

ELI: How she feels about Guido.

ARTHUR: How *Roslyn* feels–

ELI: I mean, Marilyn – Roslyn, whatever– She's the heart of this deal. Otherwise you've just got these men getting tight, messing with horses, dreaming some dreams– It's the girl carries the load, you know what I mean? She – what? Help me out–

ARTHUR: Makes them feel alive.

ELI: Exactly. Like some may say about Marilyn herself. Like sex–

ARTHUR: Or death.

ELI: Yeah. Yeah. Nothing makes you feel more alive than death.

ARTHUR: Eli– How do you think she seems?

ELI: Great. She looks great.

ARTHUR: I've got to make it work–

ELI: The deal you put together? Relax. Me and Gable and Monty. Huston–

ARTHUR: I knew exactly what the picture had to be. Frank and I walked into Seven Arts with a complete line-up, A to Z. You've got to have complete control from the beginning. It's the only way to force any kind of creative integrity out of Hollywood–

ELI: It's a damn family reunion. Marilyn's tickled pink.

ARTHUR: Did she tell you that?

ELI: Sure she is. Any girl would be. *I'm* tickled pink.

ARTHUR: If I can give her something concrete, something to hold on to–

ELI: Then make Guido a swell dancer. I mean, I realize
   asking you to rewrite may be like punching a hole in
   Hoover Dam but in the party scene out at Stix–

ARTHUR: All right, all right–

ELI: Guido can dance? Bless your little heart!

ARTHUR: Can you pull it off–

ELI: Watch me. I'll be dancing circles around Gable.
   Jesus, Miller, look at us. A couple of bums from
   Brooklyn dreaming a dream called The Misfits. And
   maybe I dream hard enough·and you give Guido a
   crack at the girl–

ARTHUR: I write the biggest picture of the year, and that's it?

ELI: Sure it is. Who gets the girl? What the hell else is
   there? And man, you'd be the one to know.
   (*Blackout.*)

Scene 3

(*The next morning. On location. Reno. A room in ISABELLE's
boarding house. On the set we see a dressing table with mirror,
chairs, and strewn about, clothes and clutter. The set mirrors
MARILYN's actual room, which we will see later. Lights on the set
are very hot. The perimeter is cooler. Here THELMA RITTER,
PAULA and ELI gather. THELMA is in her IZ costume.
PAULA, as usual, is in her black robes.*)

THELMA: The casino was going wild. Talk about the luck
   of the Irish–

ELI: Why can't it be the luck of the Jews–

THELMA: You couldn't even get close to the table. John
   had'm standing on their heads. Then this one old lady, a
   real grandmother type, has a heart attack, standing there,
   watching John–

PAULA: My word!

THELMA: They carry her out on a stretcher, and John's up
   25 grand!

(*JOHN HUSTON enters straight from Harrah's casino. He has a Danish in one hand, a mug of coffee in the other.*)

JOHN: You left early.

THELMA: You didn't! John! Where'd you end up? Down what?

ELI: Uh-oh–

JOHN: Five.

THELMA: Five!

PAULA: Five what?

THELMA: Clamaroonies–

PAULA: How can anyone be that cavalier about money?

THELMA: 'Cause maybe it's not his money.

JOHN: Money doesn't mean a damned thing. The great lesson of gambling.

(*ARTHUR enters with script in hand.*)

And the great lesson of craps is that it's random as hell, and random is the great equalizer. (*To ARTHUR, looking at set.*) What do you think?

ARTHUR: Perfect.

JOHN: Metty's throwing a few more lights in. They got it a goddam mess all right.

ARTHUR: (*To JOHN.*) Can I talk to you a minute?

JOHN: Talk.

ARTHUR: About the script.

JOHN: That's your department, amigo. Sooner we get this down the better. A few hours, and this place'll be a Chinese sweatbox.

ARTHUR: Maybe this afternoon–

JOHN: This afternoon I'm going to see a man about a horse. Iz!

THELMA: Yes, sir!

(*THELMA crosses to JOHN.*)

JOHN: You come in here, and then you cross over here.

THELMA: What's my cue line?

JOHN: Hell, if I know. Play it and we'll see.

PAULA: We worked it out. Marilyn wants you to enter on the second beat of–

(*MARILYN enters. She is wearing her costume: the famous $700 designer slip. She stands apart from the others, on the edge of the lights. She holds the script pages in her hand. In the underclothes, set apart, she seems small and vulnerable. The 'grips', BUZZY and SKIP, cross past her, running a cable.*)

BUZZY: Hey, Ms Monroe! Buzzy from *Some Like It Hot*. Never thought we'd see you in a horse opera.

MARILYN: Buzzy! I love horses, and my husband wrote this picture for me. (*Looks around.*) Eli!

ELI: Say "Hello Guido."

MARILYN: Hello, Guido. John–

JOHN: Hey, kiddo–

MARILYN: Here I am. Right on the button.

JOHN: Good to see you–

MARILYN: Long time, no see. Gosh, a real long time–

THELMA: Miz Monroe, I'm Thelma Ritter.

(*MARILYN takes THELMA's hand.*)

MARILYN: Hi. I'm Marilyn. I'm such a big fan of yours.

THELMA: Likewise.

(*MARILYN sees set.*)

MARILYN: I can't believe we're really here!

(*FRANK TAYLOR, the producer, enters. He is long, lean and urbane – the best dressed man, and the look is "resort".*)

Frank, darling, look! It looks just like my room!

FRANK: Not that bad.

ARTHUR: Frank, the air conditioner in Marilyn's trailer's not working.

FRANK: We can't have that. Anything else I can do for anybody?

THELMA: A diamond ring, a motorboat, and unlimited credit at the casino like John's got–

ELI: Go easy on him, Thel. He's new at this–

THELMA: That's what I'm counting on–

FRANK: Everyone– the Mayor of Reno has planned a party for us Sunday night. You're all invited, and then there's my party Saturday night–

JOHN: Taylor, it's your money we're wasting standing around here gabbing–

FRANK: I'm going.

THELMA: Don't forget the diamonds.

JOHN: He's a producer, not a fairy godmother. Guido! Are you in this scene?

ELI: No, sir.

JOHN: Beat it.

FRANK: Come on, Eli. We'll play a little golf. I expect my money's worth, Thelma. Break a leg...

THELMA: For a price–

(*All laugh. FRANK and ELI exit.*)

JOHN: OK, kid. Let's run through it.

(*JOHN crosses to MARILYN at the dressing table.*)

Iz comes in. Talk. Talk. Talk. Then you'll cross to the closet.

MARILYN: Where I put my dress on.

JOHN: Over your head. Is it hard to get on?

MARILYN: It's a little tight–

JOHN: Good.

MARILYN: So, then– Where am I?

JOHN: Right there.

MARILYN: (*Indulgent.*) No, John, I mean, about the divorce. Like am I happy or sad or–

ARTHUR: She's nervous.

MARILYN: I'm already that.

(*Everybody laughs.*)

THELMA: Join the club, sweetie.

MARILYN: (*To THELMA.*) You nervous, too?

PAULA: All great actresses are nervous. Roslyn knows she must perform the answers perfectly before the Judge.

(*MARILYN pulls a slip of paper from between her breasts.*)

MARILYN: I've got the answers right here. I wrote them on this little piece of paper, so she could be, like, learning them.

(*MARILYN slips the paper on to the mirror.*)

(*To THELMA.*) Arthur got all this stuff from my divorce with Joe. So it's really real–

JOHN: (*To offstage.*) What scene number is this?

MARILYN: But I don't know if she really wants it, though? John?

JOHN: What?

ARTHUR: The divorce.

MARILYN: Because, John, you know maybe, like deep inside she's not totally a hundred percent sure.

JOHN: The girl's in Reno, for God's sake.

MARILYN: Still, she's still losing something. Even if–

JOHN: Yeah. A good-time Charlie in a shiny suit.

MARILYN: She can be sad, but glad, too, kinda, like relieved, almost. And afraid. That's a lot. It's like–

PAULA: Visualize it. Put the feelings in your hands.

MARILYN: It's like– Like a fish–

PAULA: Good, dear–

(*MARILYN cups her hands, closes her eyes.*)

MARILYN: Like holding a little fish. It tickles– And flops around– Drowning. In the air– No matter what– There's no way– She holds it and it dies or she drops it and– it's gone– Yes!

(*MARILYN drops the fish and finds the emotion and she crosses to the dressing table. She sits down and picks up her lipstick and lipstick brush and she begins to do her lipstick. THELMA crosses to her mark.*)

JOHN: (*To offstage.*) Metty! Where the hell's that glare coming from? Kill the son of a bitch–

(*MARILYN reads her answers from the slip of paper on the mirror, mumbling to herself.*)

(*To offstage.*) Now you're losing her backside. I want a nice glow on the backside. At the mirror.

(*MARILYN slips off into her role with lipstick and whispers.*)

Good. Good. OK. Quiet on the set. Roll–

MARILYN: But John, just a minute. He's her husband– I mean it's still not like the easiest– Breaking the vows of marriage that she took to be so seriously.

JOHN: She dumps the guy, honey, or we don't have a picture. Roll sound. Scene 10. Take 1.

(*The slate clicks.*)

Action!

(*Blackout. Spot up on HARRY MINES, studio publicity man. HARRY is a black and white kind of guy. If he had to kill to protect his picture he would. He's on the phone with a studio Bigwig.*)

HARRY: Fucking death knell! Sure it is. Taylor out there blabbing like a Swedish maid–

(*HARRY shakes a Time magazine.*)

Time magazine says "The ultimate motion picture!" What does he think we're making here? *Gone With The Wind* meets *Spartacus*? We ain't got no story. Ain't got no action– Naw. Maybe ten minutes worth– Nothing– It ain't even in colour. Yeah. We got the words. Words we got. Horses we're gonna get. Monroe we got, sort of– And now half the United States of America is waiting for the picture we ain't got–

(*HARRY listens as Bigwig talks back.*)

Yes, sir.

(*Blackout.*)

Scene 4

(*Saturday night. ARTHUR and MARILYN's suite at the Mapes hotel. ARTHUR sits at his typewriter, typing. MARILYN sits at her dressing table working on her make-up. Strewn across the bed is a plethora of long-stemmed roses and the box they arrived in. MARILYN takes a few pills.)*

MARILYN: You gonna change?

(No answer. ARTHUR types.)

It's s'posed to be a nice party. But Frank said casual.

(ARTHUR types.)

Reno's pretty casual– And I don't want to go too overboard you know, not tonight, being like, meeting everybody–

(ARTHUR types.)

What is that?

(No answer.)

Hey!

ARTHUR: What?

MARILYN: What're you working on?

ARTHUR: Scene for Monday.

MARILYN: My first scene with Clark– Me and Paula've been working on it like crazy– So didn't John like it how it already is?

(No answer.)

John didn't like it?

ARTHUR: John doesn't seem to be that interested in the script.

MARILYN: And you want it perfect. Every little word–

(MARILYN moves close to ARTHUR, looks over his shoulder.)

They're my words– All of them. So leave'm alone– Trust me.

(MARILYN rubs ARTHUR's cheek.)

You gonna shave?

ARTHUR: Marilyn–

MARILYN: I think you better–

ARTHUR: I'm in the middle of–

MARILYN: I'm just trying to help. Remind you what a girl's like–

(*By now she is physical with ARTHUR, rubbing his shoulders or just nuzzling him.*)

Always saying you want to write the truth.

ARTHUR: I'm serious–

MARILYN: What's new?

ARTHUR: I don't finish this tonight, we won't have anything to shoot on Monday.

MARILYN: Tomorrow.

ARTHUR: Virginia needs it in the morning to make copies.

MARILYN: Virginia who?

ARTHUR: Frank's secretary.

MARILYN: The bitch with the horse face and the fake English accent?

(*ARTHUR cracks a little, maybe a smile.*)

ARTHUR: She is British. And she's not a bitch.

MARILYN: She's screwing John.

ARTHUR: How do you know?

MARILYN: I know. 'Cause he likes horses.

(*ARTHUR actually laughs at this, melting further.*)

And she's the kind of girl that likes to be ridden. Hard and fast.

ARTHUR: I thought John had his eye on that–

MARILYN: Who cares?

(*MARILYN has loosened ARTHUR up enough that he now succumbs to an embrace and kiss. They can go as far as they want with it, but as ARTHUR gets more ardent, MARILYN pulls back.*)

ARTHUR: Always when I'm working–

MARILYN: Maybe I like working men. How much time do we have?

(*MARILYN checks ARTHUR's wristwatch.*)

Not a whole bunch–

ARTHUR: Enough.

MARILYN: But then a girl has to have another bath–
(*MARILYN pulls away slowly.*)
And do her make-up all over again.

ARTHUR: There's time.

MARILYN: After the party. Promise. We need to go a little before ten, 'cause that's when Clark's coming, and we should already be there, like– Maybe I'll dress up a little, and you can wear your nice new sport coat, the linen one you look so handsome in, 'cause you're the writer–

ARTHUR: I called Frank and told him I had to work.

MARILYN: What?

ARTHUR: Get the scene done.

MARILYN: The party's for me! For me to meet Clark 'cause Frank knows I'm scared to death to. I can't walk in there by myself–

ARTHUR: Get Paula.

MARILYN: Paula?

ARTHUR: Or Ralph–

MARILYN: Oh, sure, like I'm gonna go with Paula and Rafe to meet Clark Gable.

ARTHUR: You've already met him.

MARILYN: A hundred years ago. We danced one time–

ARTHUR: There's no reason to worry–

MARILYN: You know why–

ARTHUR: He wouldn't be here if he didn't believe in you and the picture–

MARILYN: I told you– You know! My whole childhood, how my mother had Clark Gable's picture up. In a frame, even, on the wall– Like he was my father, and that's how it still feels. That's why you put him in the picture. All for me. And now, not having him all this time for real, and now him sitting there waiting for me, and I don't even bother showing up– Please, Poppy–
(*ARTHUR resumes typing.*)
Please–

ARTHUR: It's a damned party, Marilyn. Frank's going to throw a party every weekend because Frank likes to throw parties. It's not about your father–

MARILYN: Just for a little. Say hi and bye. We'll be back and you can work–

ARTHUR: After I spend three hours putting you to bed–

MARILYN: I won't–

ARTHUR: Because you drink too much–

MARILYN: I promise–

ARTHUR: And acted hot for Gable or Eli or God knows who, the waiter or–

MARILYN: I promise, I won't.

ARTHUR: I actually have a job on this picture, Marilyn–

MARILYN: What about me? I've got a fucking job to get to Frank's tonight so we all get to know each other in nice surroundings, so on Monday–

ARTHUR: Then I think you should go–

MARILYN: And they'll all know you wouldn't even do that for me, not even one tiny thing. Everybody, Monty, Clark's wife–

(*MARILYN drops her robe and stands before him naked.*)

You'll fuck me, but you won't take me to my own party at my own producer's.

ARTHUR: Put your clothes on.

MARILYN: No.

ARTHUR: Put your clothes on, Marilyn.

MARILYN: You want me. I want to go to the party. We can trade.

(*ARTHUR doesn't move or speak.*)

You wanted me.

ARTHUR: I always want you.

MARILYN: Since when? Not all these months– Or years–

ARTHUR: Not when you steal me from myself.

MARILYN: But that's what it's about–

ARTHUR: Put your clothes on.

MARILYN: And this is what I am. Like you take me away from me, and I take you away from you. I mean, isn't the idea not to be me or you but be, be something together, bigger than anyone of you and me–

(*ARTHUR stands. He turns to MARILYN and dresses her with the fallen robe. She responds to him and allows herself to be clothed.*)

ARTHUR: You're fine. You're lovely.

MARILYN: Always?

ARTHUR: You're tired.

MARILYN: Do you wish I was Deborah Kerr?

ARTHUR: (*Laughs.*) No.

MARILYN: I bet you could have written *The Brothers Karamazov* for Deborah Kerr. Would you of? I don't feel good, Poppy.

ARTHUR: I'll call Frank.

MARILYN: Tell him I'm sorry. Tell him to tell Clark specially. I don't want him to be waiting there for me. And that I'll see him Monday morning. And to thank him for the roses. He sent me roses...

(*MARILYN turns to ARTHUR. Once again they kiss. This time there is even more passion. Blackout.*)

Scene 5

(*Monday morning. On location at the Stix ranch, outside Reno. CLARK GABLE sits in the shade with his leather-bound script in his lap. He wears the costume of Gay Langland, is made up and ready to shoot. He studies the script saying lines aloud to himself. FRANK enters, striding.*)

FRANK: She's here. She's in the trailer. They're into final make-up. Thank you for being so patient.

(*ARTHUR enters.*)

(*As much to ARTHUR as to CLARK.*) It shouldn't be much longer. I'll see what I can do.

(*FRANK exits. ARTHUR approaches CLARK.*)

CLARK: I look forward to working with your wife, Mr
    Miller. If she ever gets here.

ARTHUR: She was determined not to be late for you.

CLARK: It's a hard habit to break.

ARTHUR: Yes, I'm sorry–

CLARK: My agent warned me. Garbo was the worst. Every
    damn month, thought she was going to die. Female
    plumbing's about the lousiest damn piece of machinery
    there is. I got the changes.

ARTHUR: You did? Good. I hope there aren't too many?

CLARK: Hell, yes, there are too many. But that's your
    prerogative. You're writing the damned thing. Sit down.

ARTHUR: I don't want to interrupt your–

CLARK: Took me back. Day's script waiting at the studio
    gate every morning when we'd clock in. Never knew
    what you'd get. Writers worked all night. We worked all
    day. Had to. Studio spies all over the place. Louie
    Mayer'd dock you in a heartbeat. I made twelve pictures
    in one year. There wasn't any of this lollygagging or
    bellyaching. None of this talk all the time. You just did it.
    We didn't know how the hell we did, and we were scared
    as hell to find out. I guess it depends on which way
    scares you more, talking about it, or not talking about it.
    Ones today, seems they like talking about it. Thinks it
    makes'm honest. Maybe it does. I gotta be on my toes
    around all these young guns. Young Clift and Wallach–
    Don't want to drag the picture down.

ARTHUR: I don't think you have to worry about that.

CLARK: (*Laughs.*) My agent said he'd got me a nice little
    horse picture. What the hell is this thing? Huston says
    it's some kind of eastern Western–

ARTHUR: That's about right.

CLARK: That it? Cowboys hunting down horses for dog food.

ARTHUR: The dog food is an irony imposed by society–

CLARK: Irony?

ARTHUR: – that forces an irrelevant judgement of these men. They've got space. They've got freedom. They've–

CLARK: Then the girl comes along. Now what is it about her nails an old bounder like Gay?

ARTHUR: That's just it. Because he realizes that here's a girl it's all or nothing with, exactly how he's always tried himself to–

CLARK: Carole was like that. Wife I've got now, Kathleen, Kay– it's not the same thing. You get older, don't have the energy for – the hijinx. Shenanigans. You settle for a little peace and quiet– God, Carole'd rip your damn heart out and laugh. Never give it back.

ARTHUR: Roslyn's motives are pure. She only means to give joy–

CLARK: Even when she's giving'm all the damn come-on–

ARTHUR: She's pure as the air he breathes, to him.

CLARK: This is something. I've never worked with a writer before.

ARTHUR: I've never worked with Clark Gable.

CLARK: (*To himself.*) Pure as the air he breathes...

(*Blackout. Lights up in an on-location trailer dressing room. MARILYN sits at a mirror as WHITEY works on her make-up. She guzzles coffee and is visibly nervous. On the dressing table are the roses from CLARK. RALPH massages MARILYN's feet or her back. AGNES waits to do her hair. PAULA crosses to MARILYN, her big black handbag open. She extracts several pills and hands them to MARILYN. MARILYN downs them with the coffee.*)

MARILYN: (*To PAULA.*) More. A green one and two blues–

(*PAULA hands her the pills from the handbag.*)

(*To WHITEY.*) The right eyebrow is too high. Feel how tight I am, Rafe.

PAULA: It's the air conditioning.

AGNES: Thank God for it. It'll be a hundred degrees out there today.

PAULA: You have to learn to dress for the heat. Study the nomad women of the Sahara Desert and you learn tha–

MARILYN: I can't work when I'm tight. Look at me. My face is all stretched and pinched looking.

WHITEY: Marilyn, relax.

AGNES: I'll take air conditioning any day.

MARILYN: (*To PAULA.*) Cue me.

AGNES: No, mam. Not til we've finished–

MARILYN: Agnes–

PAULA: (*Reading from the script.*) "You got children?"

MARILYN: "I – I–"

PAULA: "I never wanted children with him."

MARILYN: That's a new line.

PAULA: "You got children?"

MARILYN: "I – I never wanted children with him." Why do I say that? You say you don't want something when you know you're never gonna have it. So she's lying. She wants children more than anything.

PAULA: So into this beautiful morning Gay Langland brings you the saddest thing in your life.

WHITEY: Come on, Paula. I'm finishing her make-up.

PAULA: He doesn't know he's hurting you, but–

MARILYN: You want to bet? Expecting me to say it like it never was ever true like you're not supposed to break your heart all over again every time you say it 'cause it's only a line he's written–

PAULA: I was talking about Gay.

MARILYN: No, Arthur–

PAULA: The script is full of stuff Arthur swiped from you. He's a schmuck, what can I say?

WHITEY: For God's sake, Paula–

PAULA: But use it. Get angry.

MARILYN: At Arthur.

AGNES: Watch the hair!

MARILYN: "I never wanted children with him."

PAULA: Deeper.

MARILYN: "I never wanted children with him."

(*RALPH pulls away.*)

PAULA: Dig.

MARILYN: "I NEVER WANTED CHILDREN WITH HIM."

PAULA: Hit the anger, and you release all the energy hiding–

MARILYN: "I NEVER–"

(*MARILYN jumps up and runs to bathroom offstage.*)

AGNES: God Bless America!

WHITEY: (*To PAULA.*) You can't do this to her in the morning. We had her almost ready–

(*A knock at the trailer door. FRANK enters.*)

FRANK: How we doing? I heard Marilyn really got some sleep last night. So, what, then? About fifteen minutes?

PAULA: We only got the line changes this morning. We simply can't work like that–

FRANK: Thirty. I'll tell John.

(*FRANK exits cheerfully.*)

WHITEY: Thirty minutes.

AGNES: I'll get the PeptoBismal.

PAULA: Marilyn, darling–

(*AGNES gets the PeptoBismal. MARILYN enters from bathroom. She has been relieved of something.*)

MARILYN: I found it.

PAULA: Your call is in thirty minutes.

MARILYN: Today is the day I lost my baby.

AGNES: Pepto–

MARILYN: Three years ago today. Isn't that amazing?

(*MARILYN takes the PeptoBismal from AGNES' spoon.*)

We were living at the beach– You tuck it away some place safe, but there isn't. (*To WHITEY.*) I smudged my whole left side.

WHITEY: It looks fine.

(*MARILYN climbs into make-up chair. WHITEY touches her up.*)

MARILYN: She's sad. That's what I had to get under all that anger. Like Anger's just the guard at the gate, protecting all the little sadnesses. Like I'm not even mad at Arthur, just sad, somehow–

PAULA: Then wade through all the little sadnesses. Feel them rubbing against your ankles, calling your name. So many little sadnesses–

MARILYN: "I never wanted children with him."

PAULA: But then Gay saves you. He whisks you away.

MARILYN: I tell him he can go, but–

PAULA: But he stays, and he talks.

MARILYN: (*Laughs.*) And talks and talks. I don't get a word in edgeways. And he cooks me that sweet breakfast, and–

AGNES: And he looks just like Clark Gable.

(*Laughter.*)

WHITEY: (*To AGNES.*) Here you go.

(*AGNES steps in to finish smoothing MARILYN's wig.*)

AGNES: I heard Kay Gable's expecting.

MARILYN: You're kidding!

AGNES: I shouldn't be telling you–

PAULA: Then don't.

MARILYN: Agnes, tell me!

AGNES: She's had a whole bunch of miscarriages, so they're holding their breath. One more week and the whole world'll know. It's his first–

MARILYN: Clark must be over the moon.

AGNES: Now don't you go telling I told.

(*A knock on the trailer door.*)

MARILYN: I'm not ready.

(RALPH goes to answer door. ARTHUR enters trailer.)

(To ARTHUR.) I'm not ready.

ARTHUR: Clark's been waiting almost four hours, Marilyn.

PAULA: Our call is in twenty minutes.

ARTHUR: The call was for nine this morning.

MARILYN: *(To ARTHUR.)* Do you know what day today is?

(A knock on the trailer door. It is a COSTUME PERSON bringing MARILYN's costume: a bathrobe not unlike the one she is wearing. RALPH answers the door, takes costume.)

ARTHUR: What?

MARILYN: Today, August 5th. There isn't any reason you should remember, really–

ARTHUR: Remind me.

MARILYN: Remind you to remember, remind you to breathe, remind you to feel– Amagansett. The miscarriage. Our baby. Three years ago today.

PAULA: Actually, Arthur, we plan to use this material for the dialogue–

(RALPH helps MARILYN out of her bathrobe, into her costume bathrobe. She is naked underneath.)

ARTHUR: You don't have to work–

PAULA: She's having some valuable first-hand emotions. If we can just harness them, then–

ARTHUR: Shut up, Paula–

MARILYN: Don't take your anger out on her!

ARTHUR: *(To MARILYN.)* I'll tell John you can't work.

MARILYN: We should have buried him in a little grave we could go to on holidays and put flowers on. What did we do with him? I don't remember– I wanted that baby.

(MARILYN exits trailer, followed outside by ARTHUR, WHITEY, PAULA, AGNES, and RALPH. Suddenly MARILYN and ARTHUR are in the centre of an arena created by MARILYN's

"Family" on one side, and on the other by FRANK, ELI, JOHN and crew members, BUZZY and SKIP, who also enter.)

(*To ARTHUR.*) Where were you last night? And with whom, may I ask?

ARTHUR: We can't talk when you're like this.

MARILYN: Like what?

ARTHUR: Like this.

MARILYN: Like how about all the time? When do you ever talk to me? You talk to her. All day long, "Virginia–"

ARTHUR: Virginia?

MARILYN: Huddling all over the script like–

ARTHUR: She doesn't always have the changes.

MARILYN: Then we have two things in common.

ARTHUR: She's a secretary, Marilyn. For God's sake–

MARILYN: She's a cunt. Talking to me in that Miss Priss English accent of hers like I'm mental–

PAULA: Actually, Arthur, she has been less than helpful–

MARILYN: He likes cunts. They remind him of his mother.

ARTHUR: That's enough.

MARILYN: I'm not the one fucking some secretary.

FRANK: Marilyn–

MARILYN: I'm trying to make this picture, and you're out there humiliating me. They all know. Ask them. Virginia. She looks like she hasn't had any either for the past two years. You're perfect for each other– Do whatever you want, but I will thank you not to parade it in front of me and the world.

(*MARILYN starts to walk off when CLARK enters.*)

CLARK: (*To MARILYN.*) Ready, honey?

MARILYN: (*To CLARK.*) I'm sorry I'm late. I didn't mean to–

CLARK: You're not late.

MARILYN: I am, too, and I'm terrible.

CLARK: Listen, now, don't apologize. Not to me or anybody, ever. You hear me. You're too good for that. You're the best, and they can wait.

(*CLARK takes MARILYN's hand. He leans over and whispers something in her ear. She giggles.*)

JOHN: Break it up. The show's over.

CLARK: Tell The Chief you're worth the wait.

JOHN: (*To MARILYN.*) You just better as hell be worth the grand I dropped at the casino last night. Back to work!

(*The crowd breaks up.*)

MARILYN: (*To CLARK.*) You can spank me. I deserve it.

(*CLARK playfully pats her fanny.*)

Thanks. I feel better. Whitey, Rafe–

(*Then to no-one in particular.*)

Mr Gable likes me.

(*MARILYN and CLARK exit. ELI crosses to ARTHUR.*)

ELI: (*To ARTHUR.*) You OK? 1.35. Not too bad. We'll get a day in.

(*ARTHUR and ELI exit, leaving BUZZY and SKIP alone on stage working.*)

BUZZY: Well, now. The plot do thicken. You in the pool?

SKIP: Bet your bottom dollar.

BUZZY: Spencer Tracy picture I was workin', he goes on a bender, and it took'm three weeks to get him back. Some grip won hisself ten big ones. Huston's in.

SKIP: What's he puttin' down?

BUZZY: Five. Grand.

SKIP: She finish or she don't?

BUZZY: She finishes.

SKIP: Guess he's figurin' they spent too much dough on this dog not to get it in the can.

BUZZY: She don't croak.

SKIP: She ain't croakin'.

BUZZY: Or crackin' up. They got her so doped up, she don't know her ass from a day old donut.

SKIP: I'd help her find it.

BUZZY: I bet you would, too.

(*Blackout.*)

Scene 6

(*Mapes hotel ballroom. HARRY conducts the daily press briefing. Various REPORTERS shout questions at him.*)

HARRY: Gentlemen, shooting continues today on location at Stix Ranch with scenes involving an antique biplane flown by stunt pilot Mr–

REPORTER: Marilyn working today, Harry?

REPORTER: Is Huston working?

(*REPORTERS laugh.*)

REPORTER: Huston dropped another five grand last night. What do you say he's down by now, Harry?

HARRY: What Mr Huston does off hours is off limits.

REPORTER: Come on, Harry–

HARRY: The man's a gambler. What of it?

REPORTER: Where's Clift?

REPORTER: Anyone checked under the table?

(*REPORTERS laugh.*)

HARRY: Mr Montgomery Clift is working with horses with the production wrangler. They are at a ranch south of Reno.

REPORTER: Boys only.

REPORTER: Give it to us straight on Monroe, Harry. How come she was out those two days–

REPORTER: Is Gable ready to walk?

REPORTER: Tell us about the pool, Harry–

HARRY: I don't swim.

REPORTER: How's the marriage, Harry?

HARRY: How's yours?

REPORTER: How come Mr and Mrs Miller ride in separate cars to the location?

REPORTER: Is it true Marilyn's moved in with Mrs Strasberg?

REPORTER: Seen any rushes, Harry?

REPORTER: Yeah, Harry, is it really the ultimate motion picture?

(*REPORTERS laugh.*)

HARRY: Well, gentlemen, I was going to let you in on a little something, a certain show over in Tahoe the cast has been invited to by a certain well-known singer, but–

(*HARRY packs up his things.*)

REPORTER: Aw, come on, Harry–

HARRY: Maybe tomorrow. If you're lucky. Gentlemen, it's been a pleasure.

(*Blackout.*)

Scene 7

(*A week later. Magnum Agency photography shoot. A tall ladder, a shorter ladder, a stool and a couple of crates. Sitting on a crate is MONTGOMERY CLIFT (MONTY), a cigarette in hand. Behind him in attendance is a young man, a PLUMBER from Omaha. MONTY reaches for a blue thermos bottle sitting on the ground. He knocks it out of reach, and the PLUMBER hops to. He picks up the thermos and hands it to MONTY. MONTY takes a deep swig. The PLUMBER goes back to his watch. HARRY enters.*)

MONTY: Harry Mines! Keeper of the Secrets.

(*HARRY sees the PLUMBER.*)

HARRY: He a friend of yours?

MONTY: No.

HARRY: (*To PLUMBER.*) You'll have to leave this area immediately.

MONTY: He's my love slave, Harry.

HARRY: He'll have to wait some place else. Outta here. Go on–

MONTY: Sticks to me like glue, Harry.

(*The PLUMBER exits, warily.*)

(*To HARRY.*) He's a plumber. From Omaha, Nebraska.

HARRY: He'll have to watch his step.

(*CLARK enters.*)

MONTY: The King is here. Hey, King, what's it like to be the King?

CLARK: You walk at five, and after ninety days you get double overtime.

MONTY: Well, now–

CLARK: Otherwise you shit like everybody else. (*To HARRY.*) Harry, I've got plans for the weekend. How long's this gonna take?

HARRY: We'll run it as fast as we can, Mr Gable.

CLARK: Thanks.

MONTY: Where you going?

CLARK: Fishing.

(*The MAGNUM PHOTOGRAPHER enters upstage.*)

MONTY: I don't think I have ever been fishing before–

CLARK: Head on out with us sometime. Wash this damn dust outta your pants.

MAGNUM PHOTOGRAPHER: Mr Gable, right over here, please. Mr Clift, you're fine.

(*MARILYN enters with WHITEY, FRANK, and ELI.*)

Mr Taylor, you're right here.

(*WHITEY blots MARILYN's make-up. ELI monkeys on a ladder.*)

ELI: What about me?

MAGNUM PHOTOGRAPHER: You're fine.

ELI: Hey, I get a ladder!

MARILYN: Is it hot, or is it me?

ELI: It's you.

MARILYN: I feel like I might faint.

(*WHITEY exits.*)

CLARK: I'll catch you, honey.

MARILYN: Promise?

CLARK: I'm right here.

(*MARILYN swoons into his arms.*)

MARILYN: Mr Gable and I are very hot.

MONTY: Hey, now, wait a darn minute.

(*PUSHY PHOTOGRAPHER starts to snap a picture, but HARRY steps in and stops him.*)

She's my girl.

(*MONTY pulls MARILYN out of CLARK's arms, into his. MARILYN enjoys the flirting.*)

I'm the best damn rodeo rider this side of the Rockies, mam.

CLARK: Yeah, and he can't even remember his own name.

MONTY: I admit to a few head injuries. Nothing too major.

MARILYN: You're crazy for me–

MONTY: Crazy.

(*ARTHUR enters.*)

Crazy. Crazy. Crazy.

MAGNUM PHOTOGRAPHER: Mr Miller, I need you on that back ladder. Halfway up.

ELI: Wait a minute! His ladder is bigger than mine.

FRANK: At least you're on one, and not under it.

MONTY: Yeah, well, Clark's box is bigger than mine.

HARRY: OK, OK, Mr Gable's got a train to catch.

ARTHUR: Like this?

MAGNUM PHOTOGRAPHER: Lower.

ELI: He kinda likes being above us all. Like God.

MAGNUM PHOTOGRAPHER: (*To ARTHUR.*) Good. Right there. (*To MONTY.*) OK, Monty, put her back now. We don't want the picture censored. Marilyn, the stool in the middle.

(*MONTY's box tips over and he falls into MARILYN's lap. The others begin to get restless with the horseplay.*)

MONTY: Could I have a cherry?

ELI: Come on, Clift. Cool it.

MONTY: Now this is really comfy.

> (*JOHN enters looking sleepy. MAGNUM PHOTOGRAPHER hands him a white cowboy hat.*)

MAGNUM PHOTOGRAPHER: Mr Huston–

JOHN: Nope.

ELI: He's always grumpy after his naps.

FRANK: John–

CLARK: Come on, Chief. Join the club.

ELI: We need the dog.

> (*JOHN takes the hat, puts it on, climbs the ladder.*)

CLARK: No.

ELI: Somebody get the dog.

JOHN: Get the damn dog.

CLARK: It's me or the dog.

MAGNUM PHOTOGRAPHER: No dogs. Are we ready? Monty?

MONTY: I'm ready.

MAGNUM PHOTOGRAPHER: Miss Monroe, if you can sit up, please.

> (*MARILYN tries to push MONTY back up. They both giggle, and MONTY falls off the electrician's box he's sitting on.*)

MARILYN: Perce! Perce!

MAGNUM PHOTOGRAPHER: OK–

MONTY: I'm coming, baby–

MARILYN: Are you all right?

MONTY: Are you?

MARILYN: Am I?

> (*MONTY and MARILYN laugh. MAGNUM PHOTOGRAPHER steps behind the camera, and immediately MARILYN straightens up. She poses and her magic in front of the camera happens.*)

EVE: OK, everybody, ready?

HARRY: (*To PHOTOGRAPHERS.*) Gentlemen.

ELI: Start your engines.

MONTY: Vroom! Vroom!

ELI: Somebody cool that boy off.

MAGNUM PHOTOGRAPHER: Mr Taylor, Mr Miller,
Mr Huston. Smiles, please.

(*MAGNUM PHOTOGRAPHER begins to shoot. As she does, the
other PHOTOGRAPHERS begin to shoot. Some, like JOHN, remain
pretty static and wooden, but MARILYN and CLARK shine.
MARILYN shifts poses with ease.*)

Good–

OK, everybody quiet. It'll just take a second.

MONTY: Behold, the Misfits.

PUSHY PHOTOGRAPHER: Guy in the back, on the
ladder. Get happy, will you?

(*MAGNUM PHOTOGRAPHER hands ARTHUR a white cowboy
hat.*)

MAGNUM PHOTOGRAPHER: Mr Miller, try this.

(*ARTHUR puts on the cowboy hat. MAGNUM PHOTOGRAPHER
goes back behind the camera.*)

PUSHY PHOTOGRAPHER: Tell Stoneface it's not a
funeral.

HARRY: Watch your manners–

PUSHY PHOTOGRAPHER: Live a little, buddy.

MARILYN: He can't help it.

PUSHY PHOTOGRAPHER: How do you know?

MARILYN: He's my boyfriend.

(*With that remark, ARTHUR can't help himself. He does smile and
the cameras click.*)

PUSHY PHOTOGRAPHER: Thanks, doll.

MAGNUM PHOTOGRAPHER: Thank you, everyone.

HARRY: (*To other PHOTOGRAPHERS.*) That's it. That's
enough.

MARILYN: One more.

(*A few PHOTOGRAPHERS including PUSHY, defy HARRY.*)

HARRY: I said that's it.

(*The group breaks up. HARRY ushers PHOTOGRAPHERS
offstage. MONTY goes for the thermos and exits. CLARK*

lights a cigarette and exits. JOHN exits with hat. ELI crosses to FRANK and puts his arm around his shoulders.)

ELI: (*To FRANK.*) We've been immortalized with the gods, Taylor.

(*ELI and FRANK exit.*)

MAGNUM PHOTOGRAPHER: Mr Huston! The hat–

(*PHOTOGRAPHER exits after JOHN and the hat. MARILYN and ARTHUR are left alone on stage. MARILYN is unsteady and she has lost the self-assurance she possessed during the shoot.*)

ARTHUR: Thank you.

MARILYN: For what?

ARTHUR: The smile. We could have been here all day.

MARILYN: You're welcome.

ARTHUR: How are you?

(*MARILYN looks at him coyly. She teeters. He steadies her.*)

MARILYN: How do I look?

ARTHUR: Things are all right?

MARILYN: Paula puts me to bed every night at nine. I mean I have to almost sneak out. You don't look so good yourself.

ARTHUR: I've been staying up late.

MARILYN: Working?

ARTHUR: How about dinner tonight?

MARILYN: I – uh – I've got plans. I like the hat.

(*ARTHUR takes off the white hat.*)

No, I like it.

ARTHUR: Dinner?

MARILYN: Good guys wear white hats.

ARTHUR: I could be your boyfriend.

MARILYN: Maybe. That'd be nice.

ARTHUR: I'd marry you.

MARILYN: (*Laughs.*) Wait a minute! That's a line! That's a line from a script–

ARTHUR: From a valentine.

MARILYN: Is that what it is? I'd been wondering. Maybe tomorrow night.

(*MARILYN starts to exit.*)

But you gotta wear the hat.

(*Blackout.*)

Scene 8

(*That night. Makeshift projection room at the Mapes hotel. A circle of light from the projector grins and dances in the darkness. We hear dialogue from the film.*)

ROSLYN: (*Voice-over.*) Guido, don't–

GUIDO: (*Voice-over.*) Well, well, well– What have we here?

ROSLYN: (*Voice-over.*) Nothing–

(*GUIDO whistles a catcall.*)

GUIDO: (*Voice-over.*) Is this what they call "art" photography–

ROSLYN: (*Voice-over.*) Gay found'm in my bag and made a big joke about puttin'm up. They're old. A long time ago when I needed the money– Come on. Let's dance–

(*The film breaks and slaps against the projector. Lights come up on JOHN, FRANK, and ARTHUR screening dailies.*)

JOHN: (*To offstage.*) The one before that, and print 3 as a back-up. (*To ARTHUR and FRANK.*) Metty's getting some damn fine contrast. That white blouse or whatever is working bigtime with the hair.

ARTHUR: God, what she puts herself through in front of a camera. You can't see anything even close to right happening, and then there it is. It's all there.

JOHN: Yeah, well, talk to Metty. He's picking up some things he's not too happy about.

FRANK: What?

JOHN: In the face.

ARTHUR: Marilyn?

FRANK: I thought she looked lovely.

JOHN: Who wouldn't next to Thelma Ritter?

ARTHUR: She's playing a woman who's been through hell. It's in the character–

JOHN: Tell Metty. He's not crazy about going down as the only cameraman in the business who can't shoot Marilyn Monroe.

ARTHUR: It's not that kind of picture.

FRANK: I'll talk to him.

ARTHUR: I will.

JOHN: Amigo, let Frank handle it.

FRANK: What about the closet door?

JOHN: What?

FRANK: What we just saw up there when she's in the bedroom with Guido, showing him around, and he sees those pin-ups of her on the closet door, it's obvious that–

JOHN: Eli was damned good. Best thing I saw today.

FRANK: But the fact that they're really pictures of Marilyn– they're Marilyn, not Roslyn– it was a joke the day Eli put them up and Marilyn found them, but– when you think what it means–

JOHN: She's a whore.

ARTHUR: She's not a whore.

FRANK: Whatever you think–

JOHN: (*To FRANK.*) It was a joke. Then he put it in the script.

ARTHUR: She's not a whore.

JOHN: It's one damn shot. Less than a minute in a picture. Twenty fucking seconds.

FRANK: Listen–

ARTHUR: I'm sorry. I can't sit back and let you call my wife–

FRANK: Arthur, he's talking about Roslyn–

JOHN: Then how about getting your wife in front of the camera? She's killing us. Call's at noon. If we're lucky we have her by three with two hours sun left and Gable walking at five. Black Bart's out there handing out the pills like Tootsie Rolls– Jesus Fucking Christ– You're right. She's your damn wife–

(*ARTHUR storms out.*)

(*To PROJECTIONIST.*) Roll it–

(*The projector light flares up. Film starts to roll.*)

FRANK: John– We had a call from the casino today–

(*The projector falters, flickering on then off. The electricity fails, and the room goes black.*)

JOHN: God damn it! Taylor!

Scene 9

(*PAULA's suite at the Mapes hotel. A blackout has wiped out the entire city of Reno. In the darkness PAULA lights candles. ARTHUR enters. He carries the white hat.*)

ARTHUR: I came– She's afraid of the dark–

PAULA: We have light.

ARTHUR: Are you going out?

PAULA: Agnes and I are going to dinner.

ARTHUR: Paula, the electricity's out in the entire Reno basin.

PAULA: You're such a pessimist, Arthur. You have no sense of adventure whatsoever.

ARTHUR: What about Marilyn?

PAULA: Ralph is here.

ARTHUR: Paula– the situation is getting beyond the control of either one of us at this point– We have to figure out a way to get her through this.

PAULA: Marilyn is my student. I am here on her behalf, doing everything I possibly can to help her reach those instincts deep inside of her, to–

ARTHUR: What about the pills?

PAULA: I am not her nurse.

ARTHUR: You give her the pills.

PAULA: I administer the medication as a friend. Just like you do.

ARTHUR: Not like this.

PAULA: Just like you do. You do. We all have, because we do what we have to do with Marilyn. Now, if you would stop all this changing around of the script. She can't centre herself in the part when you keep changing it. She can't sleep for worrying, and if she can't sleep–

ARTHUR: You're as afraid of all this as I am, and you're not lifting a finger to help–

PAULA: Six years of my life I've given to her. Like a child to me. More than my own children–

ARTHUR: She has to finish the picture.

PAULA: Why?

ARTHUR: That's why she can't work– Feeding her this–

PAULA: Cutting her lines–

ARTHUR: Poisoning her against me.

PAULA: Systematically reducing her role into the periphery.

ARTHUR: I trusted you to help save her.

PAULA: Don't be ridiculous. Artists can't be saved from themselves. Maybe ordinary people but not her– She is a vessel. Entrusted to us – to me – by God Himself–

(*ARTHUR tries a door. Inside the room is dimly lit with candles or portable lanterns. It is messy and boxes and unpacked bags spill out everywhere. MARILYN is on the bed, naked, and RALPH massages her. A young DOCTOR enters from the bathroom with a ready syringe in his hand.*)

ARTHUR: Marilyn?

(*MARILYN lifts her head and turns to see ARTHUR.*)

MARILYN: Don't tell him–

ARTHUR: (*To DOCTOR.*) What is this?

MARILYN: He'll say No. He always says No.

ARTHUR: No–

MARILYN: See– Yes. Oh, yes!

(*ARTHUR springs toward the DOCTOR, but RALPH is fast and rises between them to stop ARTHUR.*)

MARILYN: All she wanted– here she could be somebody wonderful just for one time instead of listening to stupid boring men saying stupid boring things all day long, which is very cryptical since you have to do that all the time in real life, so why would you want to do it in a picture? So why–

ARTHUR: Marilyn, listen to me–

MARILYN: But she thought, well, at least your own husband could, like, be different from, from – all the ones that– But no– No–

ARTHUR: Marilyn–

MARILYN: Liar! Bastard stinking liar!

ARTHUR: I have the hat–

MARILYN: All she wanted– something wonderful– In color–

ARTHUR: It is. It is. I wrote you Roslyn with all my blessing–

MARILYN: Blessing! Wow! Your blessing. So why– Why– OK. Like how, then? You want to know what this fucking blessing feels like, your words in my mouth– Like one more dick. That's what it feels like. (*To DOCTOR.*) Do it! Now!

(*The DOCTOR moves closer to MARILYN.*)

ARTHUR: It makes it worse, Marilyn. It doesn't make anything better. You know that–

MARILYN: Get that liar away from me. (*To ARTHUR.*) Liar!

ARTHUR: (*To DOCTOR.*) Give her that, and you are culpable. Ralph! Don't let her–

MARILYN: (*To ARTHUR.*) Get out! Get him out of here this minute! I mean it! Get out! GET OUT! GET OUT!

(*By this time MARILYN is hysterical and screaming to hoarseness. PAULA pulls ARTHUR back, out of the room. She closes the door.*)

PAULA: The Doctor will take care of her.

ARTHUR: They give her whatever she wants.

PAULA: Don't we all. I've got to run. I'm glad we had our little chat, Arthur. Time heals all tempers, and sleep– Sleep, as we know, is the best medicine of all.

(*PAULA reaches into her handbag. She unearths an extra flashlight and hands it to ARTHUR.*)

You may need this. Nighty night.

(*PAULA exits, leaving ARTHUR holding the white hat and the flashlight. He stares at the bedroom door. The DOCTOR enters through it.*)

DOCTOR: (*To ARTHUR.*) Don't worry. I gave her enough to put out the entire San Francisco Forty Niners.

(*ARTHUR doesn't move or speak.*)

Go on in. She won't even know you're there.

(*The DOCTOR exits. ARTHUR slowly opens the bedroom door and enters. RALPH is arranging the bedcovers around MARILYN's still body. ARTHUR starts to touch her, then stops. He just stands looking at her. RALPH exits room softly. Lights fade.*)

Scene 10

(*End of the line. Friday afternoon, August 26th, 1960. On location, Dayton. A car sits under the hot sun, on the set. Inside the car, BUZZY works on a microphone above the windshield. Outside the car, a couple of large umbrellas mushroom. Under one JOHN snoozes, his hat down over his face. Under another, MONTY drinks from the blue thermos. The PLUMBER sits watch. FRANK sits in a canvas chair labelled 'Mrs Strasberg'. ARTHUR is off to himself, reading a lurid tabloid that hides his face.*)

(*Other labelled chairs scattered about are 'Marilyn Monroe', 'Montgomery Clift', 'Clark Gable' and 'Eli Wallach'.*)

FRANK: (*To MONTY.*) Eddie's having a little party tomorrow night. He'd love for you to come.

MONTY: Who's that?

FRANK: Eddie, my assistant.

MONTY: That Eddie–

FRANK: He'll call you.

MONTY: What kind of party exactly? A fun kind of party?

FRANK: One can but hope. Oh, and why don't you bring
your young friend–

(*PAULA enters. As usual she is dressed in black from head to toe and
carries her big black handbag. FRANK stands.*)

PAULA: This heat is monstrous. Monstrous–

(*PAULA sits in her chair. She reaches into her handbag and pulls
out a fan. She unfolds it and fans herself.*)

Why in the world does this have to be shot inside an
automobile? Tell me that. You wouldn't shoot a scene
inside a closet. Or under a bed–

FRANK: We have to leave those things to John.

PAULA: Some people naturally try to make things impossible
for everyone else.

FRANK: But they're the ones who make life interesting,
aren't they? (*To MONTY.*) Tomorrow night.

(*FRANK exits.*)

PAULA: (*To MONTY.*) You want a lifesaver?

(*She fishes inside her bag.*)

Peppermint– very cooling.

MONTY: Nope.

PAULA: (*To PLUMBER.*) What about you?

(*The PLUMBER rises and crosses to PAULA. He takes the mint
from her, then returns to his seat.*)

PLUMBER: Thank you.

PAULA: You're welcome. The Chinese chew mint leaves.
In the heat. Keeping a constant inner temperature is vital
for one's–

MONTY: Looks like you're fucking burning up.

PAULA: I'm not.

MONTY: Looks like you are.

(*ELI and THELMA enter in costume.*)

ELI: (*To BUZZY in car.*) How's it coming?

BUZZY: Getting there.

THELMA: What's wrong?

ELI: Marilyn's mike. They can't get the sound levels right. Clark was booming, and they couldn't pick up Marilyn.

PAULA: Why in the world anyone would shoot a scene inside a parked automobile–

THELMA: John's over there dreaming up new tortures as we speak. You oughta talk to the second unit guys. The ones doing the horse stuff–

MONTY: The fun part.

THELMA: Big fun. One of the stuntmen almost got his head bashed in yesterday. And our dear director, was thrilled 'cause they got the whole thing down–

ELI: How do you know?

MONTY: She's screwing the whole second unit.

THELMA: I thought you were.

MONTY: I am.

ELI: OK, you two. Clean it up.

(*CLARK enters. He is followed by his wife, KAY. CLARK wears his Gay Langland costume. He is visibly angry. He crosses to his chair and places the script in its customary place across his lap.*)

(*To CLARK.*) They're still working on the microphones.

THELMA: Kay, my dear, how're you feeling?

KAY: Fine.

CLARK: She shouldn't be out here in this heat.

KAY: I just wanted to see what was happening–

CLARK: OK. You've seen it. Now get back to the trailer–

(*KAY doesn't move.*)

Did you hear me?

(*KAY exits.*)

THELMA: See ya.

(*PAULA invades ARTHUR's territory. The headline of his tabloid reads: Monroe jilts art, film?*)

PAULA: (*To ARTHUR.*) How can you read that trash? Arthur!

ELI: He's got a persecution complex.

ARTHUR: Amazing. Absolutely amazing–

THELMA: Somebody kick John and make sure he's still breathing.

JOHN: Like hell you will. (*From under hat.*)

THELMA: He's alive. Surprise. Surprise.

CLARK: What the hell's taking so long?

JOHN: Buzzy!

BUZZY: (*Inside car.*) Five more minutes.

PAULA: This American obsession with machines– Why can't we do the scene under a tree? A tree is natural and its –

(*JOHN rises from the dead. He crosses to see what BUZZY is up to in the car. MARILYN enters. WHITEY follows her. In spite of the colour in her make-up and costume, she floats like a ghost as if she's not all there.*)

MARILYN: What's his name again. The one, you know–

MONTY: Perce.

MARILYN: Perce. Perce. Perce. How can I forget? Do I know he's not dead? Or do I think he is dead?

PAULA: You think he's unconscious.

MARILYN: But I'm still afraid.

(*PAULA reaches into her handbag and extracts some pills. She hands them to MARILYN, who takes them without water.*)

MARILYN: Afraid for Perce. For me. I forget what I remember. Do I love Perce? I do, don't I–

ARTHUR: Gay–

MARILYN: I love Gay. I don't love Perce.

JOHN: (*To BUZZY in car.*) Tuck that cord in there good. Yeah–

BUZZY: (*Into mike.*) Testing, 1, 2. Testing.

MARILYN: Perce–

MONTY: Roz–

MARILYN: Perce–

ELI: Why don't you put your sympathy where it's deserved?

MARILYN: I try– I do–

BUZZY: I'm done.

(BUZZY climbs from car.)

The heat's fusing the connectors. I don't know how long they're gonna last.

JOHN: OK, let's get it down now–

(MARILYN crosses to car. BUZZY exits after looking MARILYN over.)

PAULA: *(To JOHN.)* We know the lines.

MARILYN: *(To JOHN.)* I know the lines, John.

JOHN: Sure you do, honey.

MARILYN: I do. I promise I do.

JOHN: Just speak into the microphone, honey.

(CLARK enters the car. MARILYN starts to open car door, but ELI jumps up to do it for her.)

MARILYN: Hi–

ELI: Guido.

MARILYN: Hi Guido. Not Perce.

PAULA: *(To MARILYN.)* Don't forget to breathe–

MARILYN: Breathe–

(MARILYN climbs into car. ELI shuts door.)

PAULA: Chocolate– Amagansett–

JOHN: We need to check levels again.

CLARK: It's a goddam oven in here. How's that?

JOHN: Good. Marilyn? Find the microphone, honey.

MARILYN: Where?

JOHN: Somebody!

CLARK: Right there.

(CLARK shows her.)

MARILYN: Perce, Perce! Oh, Perce, what if you'd died–

MONTY: I'm here, baby–

JOHN: Speak up a little–

MONTY: What are they doing to you? Hey–

MARILYN: Oh, Perce, what if you'd died–

MONTY: Hey– What is this?

JOHN: Good. Good, keep it up there– Tears! We need tears!

> (*WHITEY crosses to MARILYN in car with his glycerin bottle. He paints tears on her face.*)

> (*To offstage.*) Where the hell are we on this thing?

MONTY: Chief! Look at her. What is this shit?

> (*PAULA knits. ARTHUR reads. MONTY drinks. ELI and THELMA watch. CLARK steams. JOHN drops back into his chair.*)

JOHN: What take is it, dammit!

CLARK: Fourteen!

> (*WHITEY steps away from his canvas.*)

JOHN: Quiet. Roll it. Take 14.

> (*The slate clicks. But MARILYN has already broken the take, twisting out the open car window, half falling, half leaning. Time stops, until she sits in the window, looking over the car to JOHN.*)

MARILYN: What's his name again–

> (*Her line trails off as the light catches the fake tears, too many of them really, falling down her face. MARILYN is still trying to work in the face of total abdication.*)

> (*Blackout.*)

> (*End of Act One.*)

ACT TWO

Scene 1

A few days later. A hospital in Los Angeles. Soft light up on a sepulchral scene of white. MARILYN is in a hospital bed. Beside the bed, in a chair, sits a GIRL of about 14. She is dressed in a skirt and sweater. She is somewhat drab. Her hair is light brown and wiry, almost Negroid, and gathered into pigtails.

THE GIRL: Dumb stupid idiot! This is all your fault. Two weeks we're stuck here. Two weeks! The Looney Bin. Congratulations!

MARILYN: Can't think.

THE GIRL: Don't bother. It never does any good anyway. They're gonna shut down the production. The whole picture's bust, and it's all your fault. Listen to me, Missie. We can skedaddle right outta here. You know what to do. Be her. Just be her–

MARILYN: I can't–

THE GIRL: Clark Gable's a nice man, we play him right–

MARILYN: No–

THE GIRL: He wants her.

MARILYN: My father–

THE GIRL: Grow up. Nobody's your father. Nobody's your mother. Who needs them? We got the camera–

(From under the bed the sound of tears.)

Oh brother. Not her.

(A CHILD about 6 years old enters from under the bed. She is towheaded and unkempt and as generic as an angel child. Her tears are sniffling and fearful.)

Get her out of here– This minute! Ring the bell! Tell them you have to sleep right now. They'll give you something–

(The LITTLE CHILD climbs up on the bed.)

MARILYN: She hurts.

THE GIRL: Don't we all.

THE LITTLE CHILD: My– my–

MARILYN: She's trying to tell us–

THE GIRL: Past. Over. Done with–

MARILYN: What, little one?

THE LITTLE CHILD: My–

MARILYN: What are you trying to tell us?

THE GIRL: *You* tell her. Tell her the camera will make her
feel better. Tell a camera don't have hands or eyes or body
parts. It don't yell or preach–

THE LITTLE CHILD: My–

THE GIRL: A camera don't laugh at a girl or poke fun. Or
poke anything else for that matter. Cameras always give
a girl a second chance. (*To MARILYN.*) Tell her!

THE LITTLE CHILD: (*Crying.*) No–

(*The LITTLE CHILD climbs into MARILYN's arms and she
holds her.*)

MARILYN: (*To the LITTLE CHILD.*) Sweet little one. I'm here.

THE GIRL: How about the sweatshirt?

(*MARILYN rocks the LITTLE CHILD in her arms.*)

Remember the sweatshirt? You remember. Remember
how the boys whistled at me? Walking to the bus stop,
going to school, and they whistled? Remember? How
things got better? People got nice. How it all changed?
Look at her– She's dirty. She smells.

MARILYN: She's a little orphan child–

THE GIRL: That's a big fat lie, and you know it. They kick
her around because she asks for it. She's pitiful. Name
one thing she contributes to this operation.

MARILYN: Sadness.

THE GIRL: Great! Can't live without it! Are you crazy?
The cameras– That's the ticket. Get back out there.
Work. Show'm– That's what I want. What does she
want?

MARILYN: Me.

> (*With this declaration of love, the LITTLE CHILD speaks up in a clear, sweet voice, surprisingly strong. Her words of pain contrast with the sweetness of her being, which, after all, is the nature of pain.*)

THE LITTLE CHILD: "my taste was me;
> Bones built in me, flesh filled, blood brimmed the curse.
> Self yeast of spirit a dull dough sours. I see
> The lost are like this, and their scourge to be
> As I am mine, their sweating selves; but worse."

> (*The LITTLE CHILD nestles in MARILYN's arms. A NURSE enters.*)

NURSE: Look at you. You're all awake. We can't have that now, can we? You've been so good that the doctor has some new medicine for you today. Here we go.

> (*NURSE hands MARILYN some pills and water.*)

THE GIRL: You took your sweet time–

NURSE: Before you drift off, if I could have your autograph, Miss Monroe. For my sister–

> (*NURSE hands MARILYN a piece of paper and a pen. MARILYN obliges.*)

I mean, she looks just like you. Everybody tells her. She's the spitting image. Her hair and her teeth and– Thanks. She'll be so tickled. Now it's time for our beauty sleep and lots of it. Gotta get this girl well. Sweet dreams.

> (*NURSE exits. MARILYN settles back against the pillows.*)

MARILYN: "...The lost are like this... " Miss Sitwell loved me doing that poem for her. I came for tea. To her house. I learned it specially. She said– She said nobody had a voice for poetry like I did. Me–

> (*MARILYN holds the LITTLE CHILD close.*)

THE GIRL: Well, I hate to tell you, but Edith Sitwell don't make the fucking pictures.

(*MARILYN sleeps. The LITTLE CHILD wriggles free from her dead weight and keeping her scared eyes on the GIRL, she slips off the bed and disappears under it.*)

That's more like it.

(*Blackout.*)

Scene 2

(*The reigning cabal. ARTHUR, FRANK and HARRY, stand outside the Mapes hotel, smoking.*)

ARTHUR: I don't see why in the hell we have to let him do it–

FRANK: We really can't stop him–

HARRY: Not legally.

FRANK: Of course, he is insured.

HARRY: But one must always consider the inconvenience in the occurrence of, shall we say–

FRANK: It's marvellous publicity, Arthur, and it has been keeping John out of the casino.

HARRY: The last two days.

FRANK: No booze. No gambling. He's taking this very seriously. The entire crew's got money down on him.

ARTHUR: We've got her back, and John's riding in a goddamn camel race– Do you realise what's coming up? The scenes in the bar, in Dayton–

FRANK: We'll ease her back in–

HARRY: What about a little pre-preparation, so to speak? Get her back in the saddle–

ARTHUR: What do you mean?

HARRY: Run'm all through the lines. Get it down.

FRANK: A rehearsal?

HARRY: Huston finally shows up, bingo! Everything's nice and easy, like.

(*HARRY throws down his cigarette and steps on it.*)

You're the writer.

(*HARRY exits.*)

FRANK: (*To ARTHUR.*) You can't call a rehearsal without John.

ARTHUR: John's not going to work Marilyn through this, Frank. She needs a director.

FRANK: Seven Arts has settled with the casino. The casino has promised us no more credit for John. Harry's taking care of the sharks, and by tomorrow, this camel business will be all over. Let's look at this as a fresh start–

(*MARILYN enters the street from the hotel. She is elegantly dressed with dark glasses and a head scarf. There is an ease about her that is new, but it is still a performance, seamless and deep.*)

Marilyn, my dear! Doesn't she look wonderful! Wonderful!

MARILYN: We're going for a walk like ordinary people–

FRANK: You bet! Give this girl a whirl, Miller. See you at the race–

(*FRANK exits.*)

MARILYN: It's nice out, Poppy. Which way?

(*MARILYN adjusts her scarf. ARTHUR doesn't answer.*)

ARTHUR: Downtown or the river?

MARILYN: The casino has a new marquee up– But we don't have to. I mean, it's OK– Oh, look at the lights tonight. The colors– It's different somehow. Not like the old Reno– Maybe it's me.

ARTHUR: The International Brotherhood of Electrical Workers is in town. You see them out with the missus and the cigars, ready to blow every last nickel if they have to–

MARILYN: Poppy–

ARTHUR: Looking forward to the trip all damn year. Living for it– Waiting–

MARILYN: Poppy. Stop it. Why do you have to make everything mean something? It doesn't have to be a story. Come here. Come here.

ARTHUR: What?

(*MARILYN pulls him to her.*)

MARILYN: If you wanted to, you *could* see–

(*MARILYN takes off ARTHUR's glasses.*)

Now what do you see?

ARTHUR: Colors.

MARILYN: See, and they're pretty, aren't they. Take my hand. We'll be the blind leading the blind.

ARTHUR: The blonde leading the blind.

MARILYN: You stole that from the Marx Brothers.

(*MARILYN tries to take ARTHUR's hand but it fishes for his glasses.*)

Scaredy cat. What are you afraid of? That I'm gonna pull you out in front of a bus or something– Why can't you trust me?

ARTHUR: You've proved your point. Let me have my glasses back–

MARILYN: But then you put them on and then you see things you don't want to see–

ARTHUR: That doesn't change the fact that they're still there, Marilyn.

MARILYN: Sometimes it does.

(*MARILYN takes ARTHUR's hand and places it against her face.*)

What do you see here?

ARTHUR: (*Finally.*) A girl.

MARILYN: See. That's all.

(*MARILYN kisses ARTHUR. It is a sweet kiss. She pulls back.*)

Who sent me away? To the hospital? Whose idea was that?

(*ARTHUR doesn't answer.*)

Yours? It was a good idea. Everybody can see how much better I am.

ARTHUR: We knew your doctor was there. It seemed–

MARILYN: Can you see it? Look at me. Tell me. Everybody else has but you.

(*ARTHUR reaches for his glasses. MARILYN gives them up.*)

Not with the glasses.

(*ARTHUR puts on his glasses anyway.*)

ARTHUR: (*Looking at MARILYN.*) I see a brave girl. A beautiful, talented, brave girl.

MARILYN: (*Tries to take it in.*) Maybe that's what I mean. But I don't know if that's what I am.

(*This is a moment that longs for comfort, but ARTHUR is no longer able to give it.*)

I'll try harder. I'm gonna get it right– you'll see–

ARTHUR: Which way? Downtown or the river?

MARILYN: You choose.

(*Blackout. Spot up on HARRY, talking on the phone. It's late. He wears a dressing gown and black socks.*)

HARRY: (*Into phone.*) Taylor was scared shitless, but I told him, I said, look, only way's let the girl take the rap. Lock her up, send up the smoke screen, leak it slowly to Hedda Hopper and the bitches– they're always bitin' quick for that ailin' female stuff. We get the tea and sympathy plugs runnin', then we pay the casino off and whoever else Huston's been dickin' and you're back to zero. Clift? A sweetheart. Shows up on the set every day like sunshine. Got a tail on'm, a damn rookie cop makin' triple overtime, hangs on'm like a damn queer from Omaha. But he gets the boy home every damn night. Know what he calls me? Clift– Keeper of the Secrets. Keeper of the Damn Secrets. What is it about drunks how they can nail you sometimes. (*Pause.*) Huston won the damn thing! Damn local hero. Two fucking humps. Over the finish line like Willie damn Shoemaker– You gotta love the guy. Bail his ass any damn time. Trouble is, you want my opinion, Miller can't write a damn picture you chain'm to a wall and tickle his balls with a feather. The guy's acting like he's on fuckin' Broadway– (*Blackout.*)

Scene 3

(*The next day. Location. Dayton bar. ARTHUR directs MONTY and MARILYN, in costume, for a dance scene. ELI watches. The PLUMBER lurks.*)

ARTHUR: A style–

MONTY: Yeah.

ARTHUR: I saw this with all the cowboys. They're always in control, moving to the music, with an economy of movement.

ELI: Not like me, boy. Guido likes to boogie–

MONTY: Like his old man.

(*ARTHUR takes MARILYN in his arms to demonstrate.*)

ARTHUR: But not too stiff–

MONTY: Nope.

ARTHUR: Dignified. Courtly.

MONTY: Courtly, yeah–

ELI: The Arthur Miller School of Dance–

(*ARTHUR and MARILYN dance. MARILYN is stiff, but recovers herself and follows ARTHUR's slightly ridiculous lead.*)

MONTY: (*Making up his own music, a variation of the Danube waltz*) Da-da-da-da-da-, dadada. DA-da-da-da-de, dedede. Da-da-da-da–

ARTHUR: How Perce dances tells us where he comes from–

MONTY: Dadadede.

ARTHUR: Perce is from a place. He has that, and the other don't–

(*MONTY cuts in. He dances away with MARILYN the way ARTHUR has showed him.*)

MONTY: Excuse me–

That's right. That's it– (*To ELI.*) It's a dynamic. An articulation–

MONTY: (*To MARILYN.*) A load of horseshit–

MARILYN: (*Giggles.*) Shhhhh–

ARTHUR: Good–

> (*MONTY finds a way to let PERCE dance, then he can't help himself and begins to improvise. MARILYN giggles as MONTY whirls her.*)

MONTY: Go, Perce, go. Baby, go. This is a dancing and drinking picture!

> (*THELMA enters. She is dressed up, for travel.*)

THELMA: Wait a minute! You can't be having fun. I'm not here.

MARILYN: Thel!

THELMA: Jesus, child–

MARILYN: Here I am, back from the dead–

THELMA: I want the name of this place and the phone number. You look like a million bucks.

MARILYN: You can't leave–

THELMA: Sweetie, let me tell ya. There ain't a train fast enough–

MARILYN: Thel, I don't want you to go–

THELMA: Blame your husband. He's the one that only put me in half the picture. The comic relief– Right? Now you all gotta get serious–

> (*FRANK, PAULA, RALPH and AGNES enter. FRANK carries two gifts. PAULA and RALPH carry champagne and paper cups.*)

FRANK: Did somebody say party?

THELMA: Oh, you!

ELI: You know Frank–

FRANK: Any excuse.

THELMA: You shouldn't have–

ELI: All right, we won't.

THELMA: I asked for that. I sure did. Hell, yes, you should have. This whole operation's gonna nosedive when I leave. I'm about the only voice of reason you got around here.

FRANK: Champagne!

> (*RALPH pops the cork.*)

THELMA: And Dixie Cups! How elegant, Frank!

(They all laugh and hold out their paper cups for champagne. ARTHUR holds back from the rest.)

I wish you all luck. I wish us luck. This picture deserves to be the best of the best. It really does.

FRANK: Thelma, John couldn't be here, so he–

ELI: He was ahead ten grand.

(All laugh.)

THELMA: That was my line–

FRANK: No, seriously–

ELI: I am serious– The camels have done the trick for old John.

FRANK: Thelma, John wanted me to give you this–

(FRANK hands THELMA a big package. THELMA opens it.)

MARILYN: I want to see!

THELMA: First, they tell me I'm making a picture, two women, three men. I tell'm I like the odds. Which man do I get? Then they tell me the other woman is Monroe.

MARILYN: Don't go, Thel–

THELMA: *(To MARILYN.)* Sister, I wouldn'ta missed it for the world.

(MARILYN hugs THELMA.)

PAULA: My dear, you are an exemplar to us all. Marilyn was lucky to work alongside an actress of your calibre.

MARILYN: I was–

THELMA: I only set her back a few years.

MARILYN: Look, Whitey, real tears–

(THELMA pulls the gift from the box. It is a pair of bright red cowboy boots with stacked high slanted heels, very dude ranch.)

Look at that! I wanted a pair of these ever since I got here. Aren't they the living end!

(HARRY enters with a PHOTOGRAPHER.)

HARRY: Miss Ritter– Can we get a photo?

THELMA: Sure.

(*THELMA poses with boots.*)

FRANK: John had them monogrammed.

THELMA: (*Reads boot.*) Iz. That rascal! Huston didn't show
'cause he knew I'd kiss him. What's wrong with you
people? What are you hanging around for? Don't you
have a scene to shoot or something?

ELI: Arthur hasn't written it yet!

(*All laugh. PAULA tries the boots on. PHOTOGRAPHER snaps.
Everybody drinks and is merry except ARTHUR. CLARK enters.
AGNES hands him a cup of champagne.*)

FRANK: There's one more gift. Something you really
wanted a lot–

ELI: Roslyn's wig.

MARILYN: Guido! Stop it!

(*THELMA takes second present and begins to open it.*)

THELMA: Lemme just take Agnes–

AGNES: Then I get to leave Reno?

MARILYN: No, not Agnes!

ELI: Cut to the chase, girls–

FRANK: OK, OK.

THELMA: The suspense is killing me. It's either the
diamond ring or the speed boat or what? You promised
me, Frank Taylor.

(*THELMA pulls a paddleball from the wrapping and the crowd
roars in approval.*)

Thanks–

FRANK: You're welcome. That's not just any paddleball.
This is the special *Misfits* Commemorative Autographed
Model.

THELMA: Golly!

MONTY: (*To MARILYN.*) Demonstrate!

MARILYN: No, it's Thelma's–

MONTY: You're the best–

THELMA: Teach me how, sweetie. Give me a few tips.

(*MARILYN takes the paddleball. ELI drops coins into the jukebox.
He selects some songs.*)

ELI: Any request, ladies?

MARILYN: It's easy. OK, you take the paddle up to meet
the ball. Don't wait for it to pop back.

PAULA: (*To AGNES.*) All she needed was a rest. I told
Arthur. She's 34 years old–

MARILYN: –you push the paddle up–

(*MARILYN starts popping the paddleball with amazing regularity.*)

THELMA: Somehow I think it's the body moves I'm gonna
have trouble with–

CLARK: Naw. Not this body.

(*CLARK kisses THELMA.*)

THELMA: I've died and gone to heaven–

PAULA: Where shall we eat tonight? Let's all go. Agnes–

AGNES: Sure–

PAULA: Whitey–

WHITEY: If Taylor's paying–

MONTY: (*Watching MARILYN.*) Look at that girl go!

ELI: (*To THELMA.*) May I have this dance?

(*ELI and THELMA dance. MONTY catches PAULA into his arms
and twirls her. CLARK sidles up to ARTHUR.*)

CLARK: (*To ARTHUR.*) I never was much for partying on
company time. Anyone seen our esteemed director?

MONTY: Rock and roll!

ARTHUR: (*To CLARK.*) I've been thinking about the ending.
About Gay and Roslyn in the truck–

CLARK: Somebody better as hell take charge around here
or my overtime'll bankrupt the whole shebang–

(*CLARK watches MARILYN popping the paddleball.*)

ARTHUR: At the end– There's a star in the sky–

CLARK: Look at her. You did the right thing getting her
outta this mess when you did–

ARTHUR: I–

CLARK: (*More to himself.*) Nobody knows how hard it is to do what she does. We make it look too damn easy.

MONTY: She missed! The champ missed!

MARILYN: I didn't–

(*MARILYN hands the paddleball to RALPH.*)

MARILYN: You do it, Rafe. (*To CLARK.*) Mr Cowboy Man–

CLARK: Miller–

(*MARILYN, laughing, pulls CLARK into the party circle to dance. The group watches fondly. Lights fade on good cheer, as ARTHUR looks on from outside.*)

Scene 4

(*Late that night. MARILYN's bedroom in ARTHUR and MARILYN's reunited suite at the Mapes hotel. MONTY and MARILYN ride the bed like it's a little boat in a big sea. MONTY is putting make-up (MARILYN's) on his face. They're both drinking champagne. From ARTHUR's room comes the sound of typing.*)

MARILYN: I hate people leaving. You know, the end of the picture when everybody starts leaving.

MONTY: Don't worry. There's never gonna be an end to this picture.

MARILYN: But in life, too– Thel and–

MONTY: Wreck my face, obliterate myself, and here I still am. Old and fucked. Enjoy it while you got it, mon vieux, because when it goes, it is gone. The young ones don't even remember who I was. (*Shift.*) Arthur is certainly marching his way to Zion. Where's the mascara?

MARILYN: In the drawer.

MONTY: (*Finds it.*) Brown. Good. All that truth and wisdom pounding at you relentlessly through the walls–

MARILYN: I always kind of liked it, sort of– Means somebody's home. Around, but not– You know. Right there.

MONTY: More lines for Clark?

MARILYN: The stallion scene.

MONTY: He wears make-up. He dyes his hair too. I'm gonna ask Mr Gable for a few little daytime tips–

MARILYN: Don't Monty–

MONTY: I'm joking.

MARILYN: You're not either.

MONTY: I hate people staying. That boy who's been following me around, parking himself outside my room, like a damn cop.

MARILYN: We need to talk about that.

MONTY: Why?

MARILYN: And about the thermos and you being late.

MONTY: Me! They're telling you to tell me? I mean, let's get it really balled up–

MARILYN: They didn't tell me. I'm telling you. If you'd stop putting on that damn make-up for two seconds, and listen to me, you'd–

MONTY: What?

MARILYN: I don't know–

MONTY: Stop fucking up.

MARILYN: They want you to be good. Arthur's all worried about the stallion scene, and you being hurt, and Frank's nervous about–

MONTY: I offered him the plumber.

MARILYN: Monty–

MONTY: I'm fantastic. I'm Monty. I'm Perce. I'm Perce, the Beautiful and Perce, the Damned.

(*The door opens. ARTHUR enters. He is surprised to see MONTY and surprised to see MARILYN still awake.*)

You're Arthur Miller, and I used to be Montgomery Clift. Arturo... Just the man I want to see. You know Perce. Do you think he's a has-been or a never was, or a fuck-up or–

ARTHUR: I wrote Perce to be a hero.

MONTY: A hero. My! My!

ARTHUR: Master of his own destiny in a world that decries will and freedom–

MONTY: Lemme ask you this. How big's his prick?

ARTHUR: (*Laughs, but uncomfortably.*) I don't know.

MONTY: You made him. You're his God.

MARILYN: (*To MONTY.*) You're his God. You make him.

MONTY: Actually, I think Perce is God.

ARTHUR: (*To MARILYN.*) I thought you were in bed.

MARILYN: Monty didn't have any place to go. That boy's camping outside his room–

ARTHUR: Tell Frank. He'll take care of it.

MARILYN: He's gonna stay in Paula's old room tonight. I said he could–

ARTHUR: Then get to bed. Both of you.

MONTY: It depends on how good the face looks.

ARTHUR: I mean it, Marilyn.

MARILYN: We will.

(*ARTHUR exits. The typing resumes eventually.*)

MONTY: So how big is Perce's prick? Big or little. Not in-between. I mean that's the kind of inside info you need about somebody. Especially a man. I mean, I'm going through Perce's guts with my bare hands. I'm in it up to my elbows, and I start to get something, like it's lost down inside of him, but then I pull all this shit up and it's not there. You know what I mean? Something lost–

MARILYN: You mean in Perce?

MONTY: Like the words are these little fucking shovels and you just keep digging til you get to it– So what do you think it is?

MARILYN: I don't know. Same thing inside everybody, I guess– At the bottom–

MONTY: Tell me.

MARILYN: You'll laugh.

MONTY: I won't. I never do.

MARILYN: It's just how I see it, kinda. I don't know– It's like a place. Like a tiny mouth.

MONTY: A mouth?

MARILYN: You have to kinda feel it...

MONTY: A tiny little Perce mouth.

MARILYN: With a little voice coming out of it. Not saying anything, just making a little sound–

MONTY: Whimper–

MARILYN: Sort of.

MONTY: Or a moan.

MARILYN: Yeah, more like a moan. Way down–

MONTY: It wants something, this mouth– Like a bottle or a–

(*MONTY swigs from champagne bottle.*)

MARILYN: It wants somebody to hear it, and nobody ever does.

MONTY: Nobody?

MARILYN: Nobody.

MONTY: Jesus.

MARILYN: 'Cause nobody wants you to hear it. Not doctors or people or–

(*MONTY swigs from the bottle again. Both of them are quietened by this conversation. It's almost too deep.*)

MONTY: There's only one voice inside Mr Monty, and it says PARTY TIME. Death, oblivion, they're all the same, mon vieux–

(*MONTY turns to put champagne bottle on the bedside table. The bottle tips and falls, making a painful crash. Like two children, MARILYN and MONTY stare at the mess, terrified of the consequence.*)

I didn't do anything–

(*ARTHUR enters in a rage. Drink in hand.*)

ARTHUR: God damn it! What the hell is wrong with you–

MARILYN: I'm sorry–

ARTHUR: I'm in there trying to write this damn thing!

MARILYN: I'm sorry–

ARTHUR: What do you want me to do! Knock you across the damn room? That's the only goddam language you understand?

MARILYN: Poppy, you're being rude to Monty–

ARTHUR: I have a responsibility– Why in the hell do you think I'm doing this?

MARILYN: For me.

ARTHUR: To make people fucking see. Do you know how hard that is? They don't want to, and it's my job to give them some kind of form they can handle, in some kind of honourable way, what they refuse to see, give them that– That's what we're all committed to here, what we're all working for and while I'm building it you're out there tearing it apart–

MARILYN: Poppy–

ARTHUR: You've got an 11.00 am call. Get the hell in bed–

MARILYN: I'm not tired, I promise–

ARTHUR: Then take something. Get out, Monty.

(*ARTHUR exits. Unfazed, MONTY finishes his transformation. His perfectly applied stage make-up is a fine mask.*)

MONTY: Well, mon vieux, when he stops being nice to you in front of other people, you're in big trouble.

(*MARILYN starts to cry.*)

MARILYN: Why do we do this? Why do we always have to fuck up?

MONTY: 'Cause it's too fantastic not to.

(*MONTY crawls across the bed to comfort MARILYN the way a child would, clumsily. He throws himself down beside her.*)

It's OK. It's OK–

MARILYN: It was supposed to be for me so it could be about acting, this time. And she can't do it when it's like this–

MONTY: Shh–

MARILYN: Not when it's not acting. When it's about–

MONTY: Shh–

MARILYN: 'Cause acting is all I can do–

MONTY: I started acting because it was the only way Mother'd let me wear make-up.

MARILYN: He makes it so she can't. It's his fault. Making it impossible– He thinks he's like giving but–

(*MONTY turns to the bedside table to check out the medicine bottles that fill it.*)

MONTY: Well, now, let's see here. What do we have in the candy store tonight? Some perky little Percodan–

MARILYN: Why?

MONTY: Sexy little Seconal? You sleeping or going out?

MARILYN: I have the instincts and the craft and the–

MONTY: Sodium pentabarbital–

MARILYN: She does. We do. So why didn't he–

MONTY: Stop trying to figure this crap out, you're the best. The best! Now, what do you have here that's fast and painless?

MARILYN: (*Slight smile.*) Sominex.

MONTY: Pardon me? Mon vieux, we'll be here all night.

MARILYN: I'm clean.

MONTY: Clean?

MARILYN: Well, pretty much. Since the hospital.

MONTY: What's all this?

MARILYN: They make me feel better, being there, like–

MONTY: Boy Howdy!

MARILYN: My doctor said I can learn to sleep if I can learn to relax. He says the human mind can learn to do anything it wants to, if–

MONTY: Listen, I know this place where they'll absolutely love you– Adore you–

MARILYN: No. She can't be with anybody, and she can't be alone. Just hold me. Please.

(*MONTY holds her and rubs her head.*)

Do that. That feels good. You hear it. I know you do.

MONTY: What?

MARILYN: The little voice.

MONTY: I don't listen.

MARILYN: Little boy Monty. Littlest boy Monty–

MONTY: I used to rub my sister's head, like this. Whatever is in the past stinks. It stinks.

MARILYN: But it's there.

MONTY: Lose it. Talk to the birds or something–

MARILYN: What used to work. At night. Hang my head on it like a hat. Other people's words– Not dreams or– Or voices or– These *Poems.* Like– Something, something "looks out into the Open." No. (*Remembering more clearly.*) "Only our eyes are turned/ backward, and surround plant, animal, child/ like traps, as they emerge into their freedom..."

(*MARILYN's voice trails as she is visibly calmed by the poetry.*)

I knew this dog one time. A little French poodle, at this foster house I got put in. She would lick my arms and hands and my face and all over– Wagging her little tail when she'd see me after school– And I would put her under the covers at night, and she'd lick me up my leg all the way up to you know where and then she'd lick me there– And that's how I found the place. Like magic, her licking me and me feeling wonderful. Being there beside me in the dark– Like the only person in the world who loved me– This little dog–

MONTY: My Old Man stayed home. Maybe he'd been diddling us and she found out– Who knows? She said it was for Culture. We set sail and lived in these guest house places, two weeks or a month– You'd get used to the smell of the pillows or the– the– whatever, the bathroom and she was packing up for goddam Switzerland. They had more languages there or some kind of shit– Me and Berty, we'd always sleep together to not be so afraid, and which ever one of us was not the most scared had to rub the other one's head–

MARILYN: (*Drowsily.*) Two little people in a little boat lost in the great big sea–

MONTY: Yeah, two–

MARILYN: Not, so– Better–

MONTY: Yeah.

MARILYN: And the voice can stop and everything's quiet. Like a desert– Don't leave me. Promise? Promise.

MONTY: Promise.

MARILYN: "Always there is World/and never Nowhere–"

MONTY: Shhhh–

MARILYN: Just stay.

(*Curled and quiet, they lie together in the semi-darkness.*)

You did hear it– I knew you did–

(*It feels like the end of the scene until MONTY unfolds himself and rises from the bed. He steals a medicine bottle or two from the table, drops them in his pocket. Then MONTY exits, taking a bottle of champagne as he leaves. MARILYN is on the bed, wound up like a foetus, but sleeping, sleeping. Blackout.*)

Scene 5

(*Mapes hotel ballroom. HARRY and FRANK stand in front of the press corps.*)

REPORTER: Come on– Is Kay Gable expecting or not?

REPORTER: It's all over the street, Harry–

REPORTER: What's the trouble with the end of the picture–

HARRY: (*Reading his release.*) Weather permitting, shooting resumes this morning out at the desert location with the entire cast on call. Thank you–

REPORTER: Are Miller and Monroe back together–

REPORTER: Why are they staying at separate hotels?

REPORTER: What's the trouble with the end of the picture–

REPORTER: Who ditched who, Harry?

REPORTER: Are they back together or not?

REPORTER: How come Miller checked into the Holiday Hotel last week?

FRANK: (*To HARRY.*) Let me speak to that. (*To REPORTERS.*) Mr Miller's typing was keeping Miss Monroe awake at night. His room at the Holiday Hotel is essentially a work room–

REPORTER: What's he working so hard on–

REPORTER: Something new? Rewrites?

REPORTER: What's Miller working on?

(*HARRY steps up to the microphone to rescue FRANK.*)

HARRY: Writing. Thank you, gentlemen.

REPORTER: What's wrong with the end of the picture–

(*WEATHERBY, a reporter, steps forward and approaches the podium. He is in his thirties, tall and lanky, and has that unmistakable look of a casually dressed Englishman who thinks he passes for an American.*)

WEATHERBY: Mr Taylor?

HARRY: Mr Taylor has nothing more to say.

WEATHERBY: I'm Weatherby. From The Guardian.

FRANK: God, yes! From The Manchester Guardian. Welcome! Harry, this is Mr Weatherby.

WEATHERBY: How do you do?

FRANK: Well, now, you're here. Super. Anything we can do, just ask. I'll tell Arthur. He's a raging fan of yours. He's extremely busy with the rewrites, but I know he wants to talk to you.

WEATHERBY: I also wondered, if Mrs Miller might be available?

FRANK: Marilyn?

HARRY: No.

FRANK: Your correspondence specified interviews with Arthur.

WEATHERBY: Yes– But I wondered if–

FRANK: I thought you were a serious journalist–

WEATHERBY: I consider Mrs Miller a serious actress.

FRANK: Well–

HARRY: No way.

FRANK: Submit your questions. We'll run it by her press secretary.

HARRY: Mr Miller says no.

FRANK: We're into some intensive days of shooting. Some tough stuff. But I'll see what I can do, Mr Weatherby.

WEATHERBY: Thank you.

FRANK: See, Harry, he says thank you.

(*Blackout. Sound effect of wild horses leads into the next scene.*)

Scene 6

(*Another night. Projection room at the Mapes. JOHN is sitting in the dark watching second unit footage of wild horses and the stallion. ARTHUR and FRANK watch with him.*)

JOHN: (*Watching screen.*) What a beauty! God, look at her! The legs! That's it. That's it. (*To offstage.*) Keep all of it! Good work.

(Lights come up.)

(*To ARTHUR and FRANK.*) That's what I like. A little horseflesh. A little action–

(*ARTHUR offers JOHN the script pages.*)

The end?

ARTHUR: No, the stallion scene.

JOHN: (*To offstage.*) Roll that can again. How did the backgrounds match up? Watch it for me this time–

ARTHUR: Are you going to read it?

FRANK: It's good.

JOHN: It's all good. You're too fucking good for a writer, sport. What are we gonna do about Gable?

(*JOHN flips through the pages, reading bits and pieces.*)

FRANK: (*To ARTHUR.*) Clark's agent sent John a wire. He won't accept any more script changes made after September 26.

ARTHUR: What about the ending?

JOHN: You got a week to come up with it.

ARTHUR: He should have come to me. Face to face–

FRANK: It's nothing personal, Arthur. It's just been hard for Clark to get all the new lines down, every day–

JOHN: Yeah, well, we'll soon see what kind of stuff old Gable's made of. (*Referring to script.*) He cuts the horse loose?

ARTHUR: Yes.

JOHN: He catches the stallion and cuts it loose?

ARTHUR: What Gay does is noble, and that wins her back.

JOHN: So Gable still gets the girl?

ARTHUR: I don't know yet.

JOHN: Jesus Christ, man! We're 17 days over schedule and we don't have a goddam ending!

FRANK: Arthur, this is panic writing. You don't do this kind of thing–

ARTHUR: I said I don't know.

JOHN: When do you think you will know, damn it?

ARTHUR: We've got an ending.

JOHN: Fairy tale crap–

ARTHUR: Fairy tale–

JOHN: It's too late for the old man–

ARTHUR: Then it's too late for all of us.

JOHN: Yeah, well some of us know that already–

ARTHUR: What's that supposed to mean?

FRANK: Gentlemen!

JOHN: Hook up something juicy for her and Monty. We get Gable in a tragic place, and we work it. We kill him off. I don't know. They're fucking Misfits, damn it, and she's a tramp–

ARTHUR: That's enough–

JOHN: Ask Gable. He doesn't know why he gets the damn girl.

ARTHUR: He is her only chance.

JOHN: Horse shit.

ARTHUR: He's the only one who doesn't need anything from her–

JOHN: Triple horse shit.

ARTHUR: He can take care of her, give her something no one else–

FRANK: (*To JOHN.*) We'll work on it.

ARTHUR: An ending can only be the logical outcome of the events playing themselves out.

JOHN: This is a picture, Miller. We've got images building us something up there we can't change, no matter how smart you are. Like life–

ARTHUR: I've always deferred to your film knowledge, John.

JOHN: (*Chuckling.*) Like hell–

ARTHUR: What I know about is human nature.

JOHN: Well, you got me there, pal. I don't know diddly squat about human nature.

(*JOHN starts to cough.*)

But the last thing we need around here is any more dimestore psychology claptrap. What we do need is a goddam ending.

(*To offstage.*) Roll it.

(*Lights go down and film footage of horses starts to roll. A spot on JOHN's face shows his pleasure. ARTHUR and FRANK are black. End of scene to sounds of horses snorting.*)

Scene 7

(*A week or so later. Desert location. Fragment scenes of shooting. Loud sound of wild horses squealing fills our ears, but what we see is ELI and MONTY playing tug-o-war with ropes and a contraption simulating the wild horse that should be at the end of the rope. ELI and MONTY rise and fall as they wrestle with the rope. The white dust flies as they fight with all their strength. There may even be blood. It's filthy business.*)

(*On the sidelines JOHN directs. He is more alive than at any other time in the play, a look of feral fascination on his face. PAULA sits next to him, knitting. JOHN laughs.*)

JOHN: Pull, young Monty! Pull! Yes! Facing death, both of you! Fighting death! Death! Fight, Eli! Good! Yes! (*To offstage.*) Metty, you goddam better be getting this!

(*ELI and MONTY fight the rope as long as they can. JOHN smiles and nods.*)

Cut!

(*Blackout.*)

(*Lights up. JOHN directs. Next to him is ARTHUR with a script. WEATHERBY stands behind them, watching.*)

Action!

(*CLARK is dragged across the stage by a truck. He holds onto the rope for dear life, as his body pummels the white dust crust of the earth, twisting like a dead weight. CLARK exits on his belly.*)

CUT!

ARTHUR: (*To JOHN.*) They stop and pick up the dog and then–

JOHN: What?

ARTHUR: They pick up the dog–

JOHN: That's it?

ARTHUR: They're in the truck, and there's a star in the sky, and they head off into–

(*CLARK is pulled by a CREW PERSON back across the stage to set up the shot again.*)

JOHN: (*To CLARK.*) How're you holdin' up, Gabe? Good, good.

ARTHUR: There's a star in the sky and they see it–

JOHN: It's her and Gable?

ARTHUR: Yes.

JOHN: (*To offstage.*) And that's it? Take 3! Action!

(*Again, CLARK flies across the stage on his belly, dust flying, horses screaming. JOHN smiles.*)

(*To offstage.*) Cut! It's looking pretty good, Gabe. Let's do another one–

(*Blackout.*)

(*Lights up. MARILYN stands alone in the middle of the great white emptiness. She is ROSLYN in her ROSLYN costume: white shirt, jeans, boots. JOHN directs. ARTHUR by his side.*)

ARTHUR: (*Correcting her line.*) "You're only living when you can watch something die."

MARILYN: I said that.

ARTHUR: You said, "You're only happy when–"

(*PAULA enters and crosses to MARILYN with her handbag.*)

MARILYN: I said what I said. How can I know what I said? I'm supposed to be crazy–

ARTHUR: It's the most important line in the scene–

MARILYN: Heaven forbid, Roslyn be outraged at this meaningless slaughter of helpless animals, let's make her totally deranged and make her say every word perfect! How can I know what I'm saying!

(*PAULA hands her pills from a plastic bag full.*)

PAULA: (*To MARILYN.*) She's helpless.

MARILYN: I know–

PAULA: She hates feeling helpless. Rage is her protection.

MARILYN: No, it's not. Acting is–

JOHN: (*To camera, offstage.*) Go for a long shot this time. Put her off in the distance like a coyote barking at the damn moon–

ARTHUR: (*To JOHN.*) She's missed it every time–

MARILYN: (*To ARTHUR.*) Look at me! You talk to me–

JOHN: Ready, honey?

OK, roll sound. Take 9.

Action!

MARILYN: (*As ROSLYN. Starts shaky.*) Killers! Murderers! All of you, liars! You're–

(*She dries. For a split second we see MARILYN with all the rage, but no words or voice for an outlet.*)

JOHN: Cut!

(*JOHN begins to cough.*)

MARILYN: I'm sorry, John. I'm ready now.

(*JOHN continues coughing.*)

JOHN: Where's the damn cough syrup?

(*PAULA takes a bottle from her handbag and hands it to JOHN. JOHN takes a swig.*)

ARTHUR: (*To MARILYN.*) Take a break.

MARILYN: I'm ready.

JOHN: Mrs Strasberg, you're an angel of mercy. (*To ARTHUR.*) You tried this stuff? Young Monty's special blend–

MARILYN: I'm ready, John.

ARTHUR: Look at the lines–

MARILYN: I can do this John. I'm fine. Tell him–

JOHN: You're alone out there, honey. It's you against the world–

MARILYN: He doesn't have the faintest idea–

ARTHUR: And no one else will either, if they can't understand what you're saying. Emotion is nothing, nothing, until it's articulated. Character comes from the right words, not some sort of vague emotional struggle.

MARILYN: Oh, sure! Sure! Put'm in a basket, carry'm around, and say they're yours–

JOHN: OK, honey? Roll sound. Take 10. Action!

(*In a mirror image of Act 1, Scene 5, MARILYN stands alone with her rage.*)

MARILYN: (*As ROSLYN.*) Killers! Murderers! Liars! You're only happy when you can speak up and die! Why don't you kill yourselves! You and your God's Country! Freedom! You're three dear, dead men!

(*Her rage cuts through the dust, the endlessness, the malaise, like a knife. She straightens in triumph to no reaction or applause.*)

Scene 8

(*Next day. Bar at the Mapes hotel. WEATHERBY and ELI have a drink. ELI is dressed exactly like Sigmund Freud.*)

ELI: Acting is like a mistress. All the time you're with her, it's never enough or it's too much, and you think–

(*MONTY stumbles up to the table and plants a big kiss on WEATHERBY. MONTY stumbles off laughing oddly. The PLUMBER follows him. ELI never stops talking.*)

–one more time. That's it. One more. You make a pact with God. One more job, and make it good, and I'm outta here, God–

WEATHERBY: (*Trying to stir the conversation.*) Was it Alfred Hitchcock who said it's a miracle any picture ever gets made?

ELI: Hitch? Yeah–

WEATHERBY: I take it this one's been more difficult than most.

ELI: Off the record?

WEATHERBY: Off record.

ELI: No hidden tape recorders? I've worked with drunks and pill poppers and manic depressives and Tennessee Williams– This baby takes the cake.

WEATHERBY: In what way?

ELI: Push me to it, aren't you? I think maybe we all thought it was gonna be this wonderful, important collaboration, of, you know, all these great artists. But in the end–

(*MARILYN enters the bar. She is a lovely vision, in a simple dress, looking as clean and happy and wholesome as she can. WEATHERBY stands to greet MARILYN. ELI doesn't see her and keeps talking.*)

...some of us, we're bigger than the whole damn thing and they sunk it–

(*To MARILYN.*) Say hello, Guido.

(*MARILYN kisses ELI.*)

MARILYN: Hello, Guido.

ELI: (*To WEATHERBY.*) Me and this girl go so far back we're practically blood relations.

(*MARILYN offers her hand to WEATHERBY.*)

MARILYN: Mr Weatherby.

WEATHERBY: Mrs Miller.

ELI: I'm interrupting something here?

MARILYN: Me and Mr Weatherby have a date.

ELI: Excuse me.

MARILYN: No, stay–

ELI: Hey, I got to go to work on Freud. John's letting me read for him today. *And* I got ten new lines from the Boss. He's worked up all kinds of new anger for Guido to explode into. It's *my* big scene in the desert–

(*MONTY enters with a waiter's tray and a drink for MARILYN. The WAITER is close behind him and unsure of how to get his job back. MONTY puts the drink in front of MARILYN.*)

MONTY: For the lady–

(*MARILYN smiles up at him.*)

MARILYN: Hey, sweetie–

MONTY: Mon vieux, this is the man who knows. He knows it all, so watch out. Unless you want to know–

(*ELI jumps up. He takes the tray gently from MONTY and hands it to the WAITER.*)

ELI: I think you have some dreams to tell me, meine liebchen–

(*ELI steers MONTY from the table.*)

(*To WEATHERBY and MARILYN.*) Auf Wiedersehen.

(*ELI and MONTY exit.*)

WEATHERBY: (*To the WAITER.*) Put it on my tab, please.

WAITER: Yes, sir.

(*WAITER exits.*)

MARILYN: (*To WEATHERBY.*) Eli'll be working his whole life–

WEATHERBY: It must be easier for character actors–

MARILYN: Don't say that to him! He's dying to be a leading man. But you're right, him and Thelma–

(*MARILYN trails off, but she is clearly interested in this man who seems to be sympathetic to actors.*)

WEATHERBY: Mrs Miller, let me be direct. It's my intention to write about the making of *The Misfits* from as many points of view as possible–

MARILYN: And you've been talking to everybody but me.

WEATHERBY: Regrettably. I was told you were not giving interviews.

MARILYN: Regrettably–

WEATHERBY: This is a chance for you to put on record what *The Misfits* has meant to you–

MARILYN: Gee, my big chance.

WEATHERBY: Yes.

MARILYN: My lucky day. Gosh– I guess for me, it was a different kind of– where hopefully one will be taken more seriously, you could say–

WEATHERBY: Watching you work, I was intrigued by how you are able to go so quickly into the emotion of the moment.

MARILYN: You gotta just jump. Or fall. (*Laughs.*) Or be pushed–

WEATHERBY: Into the unconscious?

MARILYN: Into the conscious! It's a very conscious move!

WEATHERBY: Which seems very different from our British stage actors. You don't often see that kind of animal emotion–

MARILYN: Animal! Only an English person would call it animal! It's people emotion! And that's what I mean– We all have it inside of us, like– It's there, and you just jump– Sometimes it works and sometimes– Sometimes you miss–

WEATHERBY: That sounds very brave.

MARILYN: See, you like focus on things. Like this little animal skull I found in the desert.

(*MARILYN traces the curves of a small object.*)

I thought it was a sea shell, 'cause it was so smooth, and like from when it was the ocean, but then I could see the eyeholes and a little mouth. These are the clues, if you look– see?

WEATHERBY: Clues?

MARILYN: To what's really at the bottom. Waiting–

(*WEATHERBY tries to regain control of the interview.*)

WEATHERBY: Mrs Miller, what has it been like working with your husband?

MARILYN: Say. I thought you were a nice man–

(*MARILYN takes WEATHERBY's hand. She places the shell/skull inside it. She folds his fingers over.*)

This'll remind you–

WEATHERBY: To be brave?

MARILYN: Yes! Take it.

WEATHERBY: Thank you.

MARILYN: They're all these poor people out there who can't let themselves take anything from anybody. And you know you have to take–

WEATHERBY: Take? Does that mean receive?

MARILYN: You know, like it's more blessed to receive than to give. All people want to do is give, and that's the easy part– Do you mind us talking about love?

WEATHERBY: (*Being very brave.*) Not at all.

MARILYN: Me neither.

(*Blackout.*)

Scene 9

(*Late at night. HARRY on the phone.*)

HARRY: Yeah, they got an ending. We shoot tomorrow. Hell, if I know... Yes, sir. Thank you, sir. Resourceful thinking.

That's the key. Turn your negatives to positives. Learned that from my fourth grade teacher. A holy sister. May she rest in peace. Listen– Listen to this– I gotta read you something– (*Reading from a newspaper.*) 'Acquaintances of Marilyn's think one of the reasons she fell for Montand–' The frenchy she was making that other picture with– 'She fell for Montand was because he resembled Joe DiMaggio. If you put Montand, DiMaggio and Miller in baseball suits and sent them out to left field you wouldn't be able to tell them apart.' Ain't that the truth! (*Laughs.*) God, I love the fucking truth, sir!

(*Blackout.*)

Scene 10

(*November 4, 1960. A Hollywood studio. Cables crisscross the floor. There are lights and other items of indoor film making equipment. Centre stage is a dummy truck cab. MARILYN and CLARK sit inside it. Outside, JOHN directs the scene. BUZZY and SKIP are under the truck cab to jiggle it so it looks like it's moving. MARILYN is snuggled against CLARK, who "drives". The last scene has just been spoken.*)

JOHN: Cut and wrap!

(*ARTHUR enters, somewhat dazed. BUZZY and SKIP help MARILYN and CLARK from the car. They exit.*)

ARTHUR: (*To JOHN.*) One take?

ASSISTANT DIRECTOR: (*On loudspeaker.*) Wrap party in the canteen! Everyone!

(*BUZZY and SKIP work. FRANK enters jauntily.*)

FRANK: (*To ARTHUR and JOHN.*) We did it! A work of art! Proud to have my name on it– We'll see you two at the party–

ARTHUR: I–

JOHN: Hell, no.

FRANK: Stop by for a minute. You owe it to the crew.

(*FRANK exits to party.*)

SKIP: (*To BUZZY.*) Who picked it up?

BUZZY: You don't wanta know–

SKIP: Sure I do. Who?

JOHN: Me.

BUZZY: Metty pulls his name out a damn hat–

SKIP: Huston!

BUZZY: Ten Grand!

SKIP: Since when the director walks with the crew's pool? It was rigged!

JOHN: Absolutely. Part of my compensation, boys.

  (*BUZZY and SKIP exit, hauling cables.*)

  (*To ARTHUR.*) Well, amigo, don't think it'll ever play Peoria. Do you? You ever get it right?

ARTHUR: What?

JOHN: The ending. You never do get it right, kid. Nobody does. Not the ending. Don't even try. Always have something else waiting–

  (*ELI and MONTY enter, dressed in street clothes.*)

ELI: (*To MONTY.*) Jesus, Clift, he cast you? You're Freud? No way–

MONTY: I admit I'm fucked up. Know what I mean Eli?

ELI: John–

MONTY: You don't have to see the bottom to swim, but you gotta know it's there–

JOHN: Hell, Eli, he's more fucked up than all of us.

  (*HARRY enters.*)

HARRY: Freud meets the press. 15 minutes. Conference Room B.

  (*HARRY, ELI, MONTY and JOHN exit.*)

JOHN: Let's go, kiddo–

ELI: Hey, does Freud got any brothers? John, I can be a patient–

  (*CLARK and KAY enter.*)

CLARK: Miller! Thanks again! An old man sure likes to know what he's made of before he checks out. You know, you get tired of all the old stuff. Do it without thinking– Not that I'm ashamed of anything I've done, but this was different. Something to put down for posterity. For the kid.

(*ARTHUR leans to KAY and kisses her cheek.*)

Heading out for some duck hunting. You oughta come along. Bring Marilyn–

ARTHUR: Thanks.

CLARK: Forty days over schedule! What Mayer would have done to us! God–

(*Laughing, CLARK exits with KAY. PAULA enters. She's in a hurry to get to the party and only speaks to ARTHUR in passing.*)

PAULA: John asked Marilyn to play Sigmund Freud's wife– John-Paul Sartre wrote the script. Imagine that! All kinds of doors are going to be opening for Marilyn–

(*MARILYN enters. She is dressed for going away, in casual clothes.*)

PAULA: (*To MARILYN.*) Don't be long, my dear–

(*PAULA exits. MARILYN stands in silence, and ARTHUR doesn't move.*)

MARILYN: Hey– (*Finally.*) So crazy how they call it a sound stage, and it's the quietest place in the world. That first time, the very first, I ever saw you– Remember? I was crying, and you heard me, on that empty sound stage. Johnny'd died, and I'd run off– I was making– I don't remember– *Love Nest* or? And you were there. It was dark and you heard me crying. You found me. And I looked up–

ARTHUR: I gave you a handkerchief.

MARILYN: You handed it to me– And here we are, like a great big circle. Only–

ARTHUR: John wants me to stick around and help him with the editing.

MARILYN: Sure.

ARTHUR: What about you?

MARILYN: We're leaving in the morning. It's OK. I mean, it really is. Really–

ARTHUR: Marilyn–

MARILYN: Look at you, acting so surprised; all the time knowing how it would turn out–

ARTHUR: No–

MARILYN: 'Cause you were writing it–

ARTHUR: Not us–

MARILYN: And me. Sure you did. You wrote me. And I took it, and we finished. It's OK.

(MARILYN starts her exit, then stops.)

"Work of the eyes is done, now
go and do heart-work
on all the images imprisoned within you; for you
overpowered them: but even now you don't know them."

Gee– I guess that's how I would write you. If I could of. If you could take it– Call me sometime–

(MARILYN exits. ARTHUR is left alone on the stage desert. Lights fade. Curtain.)

WINDING THE BALL

a divine comedy in two acts

For Gus and Juliet

CHARACTERS

DEEMER

LEONA

CLAUDE

JANNIE LAMBERT

ROBB LAMBERT

FATHER

TOWN COP

BREAD MAN

TROOPER

JAM JAR LADY

MRS GUANZO

Winding The Ball was first performed at the Royal Exchange Theatre, Manchester on the 26th October 1989, with the following cast:

DEEMER, Ian Bartholomew
LEONA, Roberta Taylor
CLAUDE, Trevor Cooper
JANNIE LAMBERT, Lisa Eichhorn
ROBB LAMBERT, David Schofield
FATHER, Gordon Case
TOWN COP/
BREAD MAN/TROOPER, Marcus Eyre
JAM JAR LADY, Sydnee Blake
MRS GUANZO, Ling Tai

DIRECTOR, Gregory Hersov
SET DESIGNER, Mike Taylor
COSTUME DESIGNER, Sophie Doncaster
LIGHTING DESIGNER, Rick Fisher
SOUND DESIGNER, Tim McCormick

The first American production of *Winding The Ball* was performed at the New York City Fringe Festival by Burning Coal Theater Company (Jerome Davis, Artistic Director/Simmie Kastner, Managing Director) of Raleigh, North Carolina, August 1998.

Place: A Farm Bureau Co-op store in the
Appalachian Mountains, South western Virginia.
Time: Now.

Note: *Winding The Ball* is a play of different voices.
It is important that Jannie and Robb do not sound
Southern or Appalachian. They are outsiders.

ACT ONE

Friday morning 7.30 am, All Saints Day, November 1. A farm co-operative store in the Appalachian mountains. Shelves are stocked with every kind of thing: groceries, clothing, tools, feed and seed, mops, farm supplies and equipment. Up front, near the check-out counter, is a display of Halloween candy and a big plastic rotating rat with red light bulb eyes advertising RoDo-DeMo rat poison. Towards the back of the store is the heavy door of a meat/beer/cold foods cooler. There's nothing quaint about this place. The jumble of it has a kind of menace – of things lost forever on the back of shelves and never found.

DEEMER, the butcher and bag boy, is eating Hardee's Biscuits'n'Gravy from a styrofoam container. TOWN COP is examining the broken glass panels on either side of the co-op's front door. LEONA, the cashier, is in a swivit.

TOWN COP: That's what they did, all right. They busted in.

DEEMER: Looks like it, don't it?

TOWN COP: Come right on in.

DEEMER: Sure did.

TOWN COP: Same thing every Halloween. I'll be running my tail off for two days complaints we got, and then the big ball game with Castlewood tonight and that's bound to be trouble.

LEONA: Show me where the Bible says one word in it about trick or treat. I ain't never seen it.

TOWN COP: You heard what the kids done down to the funeral home last night? One of them caskets, one of them bronzed ones with detailing on the sides, costs as much as a new car, and what they did was put an old stray dog inside it and closed the thing up and if some-body hadn't of heard it barking the dog would of died in it and Wish says as it is he'll have to mark the casket down at least half price if they can ever get the dog shit out of it, all over the white silk lining. (*Pause.*) But you said everything looks all right? Nothing been took?

DEEMER: Don't seem to be

TOWN COP: Every damn Halloween. Pardon me.

DEEMER: But you thinking it was just kids.

TOWN COP: Probably just wanting a pop or a cake. Where's the cash?

(*DEEMER takes a workboot off the shelf and out of it pulls a zippered cashbag. He opens it and checks inside.*)

LEONA: Arrest them all! Lock them on up! All them sitting in the shade by the post office day in, day out.

(*DEEMER hands the cashbag to TOWN COP.*)

TOWN COP: All there?

DEEMER: I'd say.

LEONA: Passing the bottle hand to hand day and night.

TOWN COP: You all make a deposit last night?

DEEMER: Nope.

TOWN COP: And this is it?

LEONA: That's for two days, too.

TOWN COP: That new K-Mart is eating you all alive. Selling stuff nobody needs, that's how you make it these days. (*Pause.*) What else mighten them kids of been after, you think?

(*DEEMER puts the cash bag back in the boot.*)

DEEMER: Got a case of Timexes back there but they ain't been touched.

TOWN COP: Chain saws, power tools?

DEEMER: We got us a tiller or two.

TOWN COP: Them boys ain't looking for no garden tiller. What about the office?

DEEMER: Nothing in there but a bunch of papers.

LEONA: Bills.

TOWN COP: No checkbook?

DEEMER: Manager's got it with her.

LEONA: Overdrawn most likely.

TOWN COP: What they did was bust this glass through and stick their hand in and open the door from the inside. Look at that thing, Deemer, it ain't got but two old granny screws holding it up there. Get you a new lock on that door.

LEONA: Shouldn't of been us here first in the first place, but on account of her being late we was here first.

TOWN COP: And the door was standing open?

LEONA: I ain't saying another word.

DEEMER: Might of been. We come in the back, us and Claude, and then we seen the glass on the floor up here.

LEONA: Let her be the one to say. She's the one should of been here.

TOWN COP: Who's that?

DEEMER: New manager. Coach's wife.

TOWN COP: Oh, yeah, Mrs Lambert. How's she working out, anyway?

DEEMER: She put a mirror up in the toilet.

TOWN COP: Took them long enough finding a new manager for this place.

LEONA: Two months and a day.

TOWN COP: Weren't paying worth spit is what I heard.

DEEMER: Mrs Lambert gives us a half hour dinner break, too.

LEONA: And calls it lunch. It takes me all of ten minutes eat my vienny sausage.

DEEMER: And she had us clean out the upstairs where we keep the feed and fix them windows where pigeons get in.

LEONA: There you go, and bringing in her own husband on a Saturday his day off to come down here and help you and Claude clean out up there and him having to bring in the babies with him for me to watch on our busy day.

DEEMER: Coach didn't mind.

LEONA: Tell me he didn't mind, close-mouthed as he was, zipper-lipped across his face. (*Pause.*) Leastways a man can be civil. Hardly a word. She were any kind of manager she would have gotten one of them boys hang out by the post office and come up and help you and Claude for a few dollars, that's what.

DEEMER: Leona don't like Mrs Lambert because she wears pants and make-up on her face.

LEONA: What she wears is between her and Jesus.

TOWN COP: You all called her yet?

DEEMER: Leona did.

LEONA: Sitter said she was on her way. (*Pause.*) Where she is is late.

(*CLAUDE enters from the back. He wears camouflage clothes and army boots.*)

TOWN COP: Hey, Claude.

CLAUDE: Hello.

DEEMER: 'Bout to get it done?

CLAUDE: Yes.

(*CLAUDE gets himself two honey buns and puts his money on the counter.*)

DEEMER: He lifting a finger to help you?

CLAUDE: No.

LEONA: That's 'bout the sorriest driver they ever send. Never lifts one finger help unload the truck, does he, Claude?

CLAUDE: No.

DEEMER: Never do.

CLAUDE: No.

(*CLAUDE exits to the back.*)

TOWN COP: What's Claude make of Mrs Lambert?

DEEMER: I told him she was Coach's wife and Claude likes Coach right much but he won't pay her no mind.

TOWN COP: Give old Claude time.

LEONA: I'll tell you what: limited as he is, Claude knows seven o'clock don't mean no quarter to eight.

TOWN COP: I got to get me some breakfast. Less there's something missing all you got here is a breaking and entering and we don't even know they entered and of a Halloween night that won't get you to the commode and back. I were you, Deemer, I'd get this hole patched up before some old boy cuts hisself and sues your ass. And change that lock. I'll be over to Doc's you need me.

DEEMER: Putting money down on the big game tonight?

TOWN COP: You ever seen Doc's grin that wide, way them bets is flying?

DEEMER: I put me down my five.

TOWN COP: Who on?

DEEMER: Coach.

TOWN COP: Castlewood's seven and o.

DEEMER: So's Coach.

TOWN COP: Explain to me how Coach's been popping it out with that pack of runts he's got. He's got those boys playing some football.

DEEMER: Coach'll be putting us on the map.

TOWN COP: Yeah, but Castlewood's got niggers. All them niggers living just over the line and the county bussing them all over to Castlewood schools. Coach had any real sense, he'd get the county to give us some nigger boys, big ones, too. (*Pause.*) Tell Mrs Lambert you all find out anything missing, give us a call. We'll do what we can, not there's a whole lot we can do, but we'll be glad to do it.

(*TOWN COP exits out front door, LEONA locks it behind him and crosses to Halloween candy display. She takes the candy from the display and loads it into a grocery cart.*)

LEONA: All this nonsense and the feed truck coming in.

DEEMER: Truck was early.

LEONA: Waltzing in here late of a morning, big smile on her face like working for a dress shop 'fore she was married means something to nobody but herself.

DEEMER: I wonder how come she didn't get her a job up to the K-Mart? They was hiring.

LEONA: K-Mart trains you, too. They trained my little
sister good. (*Pause.*) I had me a husband with two good
lungs working and me two girl babies at home, I tell you
where I'd be and it wuddent be in no K-Mart store.

DEEMER: (*Pause.*) She likes what it smells like in here.

LEONA: Mercy!

DEEMER: Mrs Lambert told me she come in here the first
time and breathed in real deep and got this smell.

LEONA: She talked to you about a smell?

DEEMER: Said it was a good smell, everything kind of
converging up.

LEONA: I'll tell you what's the truth, you won't find a smell
up at K-Mart, they're too smart for that. Why aren't you
back there helping Claude?

DEEMER: 'Cause Friday's my biscuit and gravy day.

LEONA: Some people have to work getting their paycheck.

DEEMER: The sum total of life and all our needs and
dreams. Right here. This place. That's what she said it
smelt like.

LEONA: The Lord Jesus Christ Almighty Everlasting
Today and Evermore is the total sum of life and he
doesn't have a smell. Talking to you about a smell. I'll
tell you why she took this job.

DEEMER: Why?

LEONA: Throwing it back in his face.

DEEMER: Why?

LEONA: I ain't saying.

DEEMER: Why?

LEONA: You know why. Mammon.

DEEMER: Mammon?

LEONA: Root of all evil and wedded discord.

DEEMER: But I'd say Coach makes right much. The county
pays good money, and a winning season gets him extra.

LEONA: For some there's never enough.

(*CLAUDE enters from the back with an invoice.*)

DEEMER: You all done?

LEONA: Don't look at me. I ain't signing.

DEEMER: Here.

CLAUDE: No signing. The driver said he must be paid today.

DEEMER: Mrs Lambert ain't here yet.

CLAUDE: The driver was very specific.

DEEMER: Then he can take hisself over to Doc's and get hisself a cup of coffee and wait on her.

CLAUDE: You want him to go to Doc's?

DEEMER: Tell him.

CLAUDE: And if the son of a bitch doesn't like it, he can load up his three hundred fucking bags of horse and mule and–

DEEMER: Lord, Claude, don't say that. Come on.

(*CLAUDE and DEEMER exit to the back. LEONA starts to follow them with grocery cart full of Halloween candy but is stopped by a knock on the door.*)

LEONA: We ain't open yet. Can't open up til the manager gets here.

JANNIE: (*Offstage.*) Leona!

(*LEONA crosses to front door. She lifts the shade to see who it is, then opens the door. JANNIE LAMBERT enters carrying an armload of account books, papers and files.*)

Hi. Here, take this. I've got more in the car.

(*JANNIE steps on broken glass.*)

What happened here?

(*JANNIE exits back out front door. LEONA carries in the papers as if they were a dead animal and dumps it all on the check-out counter. JANNIE enters with another armload, her sack lunch and purse and a coffee maker and whatever else.*)

JANNIE: Did you see the mountains this morning, Leona?

LEONA: No.

JANNIE: The mists rising up from the hollows and getting snagged on the mountain tops – I love mornings like this. I brought the coffee maker. Do you drink coffee? I was going to work on the books last night but I had to take the girls trick or treating so I didn't even get to it and I thought I'd better bring it all back in today in case I got time to work on it here. Would you believe I left my key to the co-op on my other key chain which is sitting at home on the kitchen counter. I've got to remember to move it to the key chain I've got my car keys on. Thank God you're here. Deemer drinks coffee doesn't he?

LEONA: Deemer and me and Claude have been here since seven.

JANNIE: Good for you.

LEONA: Punched in at seven-o-three.

(*Sound effect of a freight elevator ascending.*)

JANNIE: Fridays are a total zoo at our house. It's a miracle I'm here in one piece. Robb had a football sleepover at the gym last night to psych the boys up, and I swear the sitter only gets migraines on Fridays.

LEONA: The truck's here and the chicken necks weren't on it.

JANNIE: The truck! Oh, my God, Leona, the truck! How could I forget. I wrote it down. I am so sorry.

LEONA: Driver needs paying.

JANNIE: Sure. Is that the procedure?

LEONA: Some drivers you pay and some you don't.

JANNIE: How do I know which is which?

LEONA: Them that ask is ones get paid. Most send you a bill but there's some don't.

JANNIE: But there's no standard policy?

LEONA: I couldn't say. You better ask somebody.

JANNIE: Let me put it on my list.

(*DEEMER enters from the back with a small cardboard box in his hands. RoDo-DeMo is printed on the side.*)

DEEMER: Mornin', Miz Lambert.

JANNIE: Good morning, Deemer. I brought a coffee maker
  for us. Is this the invoice for the horse and mule feed?

DEEMER: Yes, mam.

JANNIE: I am so sorry I'm late. You wouldn't have believed
  my house this morning. Deemer, run out and see if I left
  the checkbook in my car.

  (*DEEMER exits out front door. JANNIE rifles through the things
  she carried in looking for the checkbook.*)

LEONA: Some kids broke in last night. Up front there.

JANNIE: Where the broken glass is? Did they take anything?

LEONA: Troublemakers of a Halloween is all.

JANNIE: I'm sure I had the checkbook with me. (*Pause.*)
  Maybe I didn't take it home. Did you call the police?

  (*JANNIE exits to office with the coffee maker. DEEMER enters
  from front door. LEONA examines the dead mice box.*)

DEEMER: The man said that it'll hold up to twenty-five
  mice or eight rats depending on size and I got ten of them
  suckers dead as Monday's hambone. Them mice walk by
  and smell this cheese smell on the poison and they go in
  this little hole and eat it and they can't get back out and
  their guts explode inside their skin while they're sitting
  there waiting to get out, but you can't see nothing.

LEONA: They high?

DEEMER: Four ninety eight guaranteed or money back.

LEONA: I'll get me one and momma, too. Remind me.

  (*LEONA exits to the back pushing the grocery cart full of Halloween
  candy. JANNIE enters from office.*)

JANNIE: Leona?

DEEMER: She's in the back. I looked but I didn't see no
  checkbook.

JANNIE: The cashbag's gone. The safe doesn't look like it
  was broken into but the cashbag's not inside.

DEEMER: No, mam, because yesterday you left 'fore
  closing and none of us works the safe.

  (*DEEMER crosses to the shelf of workboots and from the boot pulls
  the cashbag.*)

Tuesday, Thursday, Saturday we put it in the size 14½ workboot steel toe reinforced. We only got the one pair. Monday, Wednesday, Friday it's in the lard bucket back of the shelf.

JANNIE: O, thank God. I about had heart failure.

DEEMER: Everybody'd know money's in the safe. First place they'd look.

(*JANNIE opens cashbag and counts the money.*)

A lock don't mean nothing.

(*Sound effect of freight elevator descending. CLAUDE enters from elevator with a dolly full of feed bags.*)

JANNIE: Good morning, Claude. Is that our long awaited horse and mule feed, I hope?

DEEMER: If somebody means to get at something, a lock don't mean nothin.

JANNIE: Deemer, go see if we have enough chicken feet left to keep the special on. We've got that ad running in this week's paper.

(*DEEMER exits into the meat cooler. JANNIE finishes counting money. She puts some of it back in the bag and leaves it for LEONA. She starts to exit back to office. But sees CLAUDE unloading bags near front door.*)

(*To CLAUDE.*) It might get in the way if we put it there, Claude. I think maybe we should just put all of it in that space upstairs you and Deemer and Robb made so nice and clean for me.

(*JANNIE exits to office. CLAUDE keeps unloading bags. From inside the cooler DEEMER knocks to be let out. LEONA enters from back pushing an empty grocery cart.*)

LEONA: Claude you better hurry up and get that feed cleared out of the back. It's blocking the restroom door, and I took me a laxative last night.

(*CLAUDE ignores the knocking and exits to back. LEONA crosses to cooler.*)

I'm coming!

(*LEONA lets DEEMER out of cooler.*)

DEEMER: Somebody hid them chicken necks.

LEONA: Big blue tub in the corner. Why do I have to know everything?

(*DEEMER exits back into cooler. LEONA goes to cash register. Distastefully, she unzips the cashbag and gingerly puts money into the cash register. JANNIE enters from office with the invoice in hand.*)

JANNIE: Can I give the driver cash?

LEONA: Checks only even if we had that kind of cash which we don't.

JANNIE: I guess I left the checkbook at home. I think I can see it in my mind, right there on the kitchen counter next to the keys. I had everything right there to take with me (I always do that the night before) and I thought I picked everything up, but I guess I didn't.

(*DEEMER knocks from inside cooler.*)

This afternoon I think we all need a lesson using the safe properly.

LEONA: What safe?

JANNIE: In the office. It's a good habit to get into.

LEONA: No, mam.

JANNIE: Why not?

LEONA: I don't touch money.

JANNIE: Leona, you're the cashier.

LEONA: I'm not touching no cashbag or no safe. Not mammon, no mam. I don't touch no bill bigger than a fifty and I don't take bingo money. Your preacher knows I don't, too. We better just get it straight right now.

JANNIE: Is there someone in the cooler?

LEONA: Deemer is.

(*JANNIE lets DEEMER out.*)

DEEMER: Cooler door's sticking again.

JANNIE: Oh, I'm sorry. It's on my list. (*Pause.*) We can't do that, Leona. Black, white, Jews or Christians or bingo players or whatever. You have to take their money. Now, I can understand if we didn't have change for a fifty–

DEEMER: We don't have to worry about no black or
    Jewish around here.

JANNIE: Deemer, go check the chicken necks.

DEEMER: I already did. Got ten pounds and some left.

JANNIE: Then go get Claude and let's look at the clock.
    (*DEEMER exits into the back.*)
    Leona, this is serious. For one thing, it's against the law.
    It is discrimination. I know you are used to doing things
    your own way, and I respect that, and it gives the co-op
    its charm, and I'm trying to learn. A lot of things I won't
    change, but some things will have to change. We cannot
    keep cash overnight in a boot. And we cannot refuse a
    customer's money.

LEONA: I go by the law of Jehovah.

JANNIE: I'm talking about federal law. We could be sued.

LEONA: Lord Jesus is my witness.

JANNIE: But we'll also have to remember Jesus ate with
    the Pharisees.

LEONA: And he spit on their money.

JANNIE: He did?

LEONA: It's in my Bible. In red letters. Jesus spat. John 9:6.
    (*DEEMER and CLAUDE enter from back with ladder. CLAUDE
    climbs up to take the clock down while DEEMER holds the ladder.
    JANNIE sees the empty Halloween candy display.*)

DEEMER: I made my bet we'd beat Castlewood tonight.
    Claude did, too.

JANNIE: Good. Where's the Halloween candy?

LEONA: In the back.

JANNIE: Let's mark it down today.

LEONA: We don't do that, we save it for next year.

JANNIE: You save Halloween candy for a year and then
    bring it back out again.

DEEMER: Christmas and Thanksgiving nobody wants
    candy with witch faces on it.

JANNIE: And the candy we were selling was last year's candy?

LEONA: I'd say some was. We put the last year's candy up top so it gets sold first. We don't want to be selling no two year old candy.

JANNIE: Put the candy back up here and we'll mark it down. Way down. Deemer, you can make a sign.

(*LEONA exits to back with grocery cart. JAM JAR LADY enters from front door.*)

JAM JAR LADY: You all got slop buckets?

DEEMER: Yes, mam.

JAM JAR LADY: I'll be back.

(*JAM JAR LADY exits out front door. DEEMER hands JANNIE the clock.*)

DEEMER: See, there ain't no way of changing the time. You look.

JANNIE: There has to be a way. Open up the back.

DEEMER: It ain't that kind of clock. It's just made to give one kind of time, and you got to adjust yourself.

JANNIE: There are bound to be directions to it somewhere, maybe in the office. Have you looked?

DEEMER: You want it back up?

JANNIE: Deemer, that clock is eight minutes slow.

DEEMER: And in daylight savings, it's an hour and eight minutes slow. You don't much notice after a while.

JANNIE: Don't put it back up.

DEEMER: (*To CLAUDE.*) She don't want it back up.

(*JANNIE takes the clock and puts it face down on the checkout counter by the dead mouse box and all her other clutter.*)

JANNIE: I'll get us a new clock. I'll put it on my list. We better get the store opened.

(*CLAUDE leans the ladder against the wall and exits to back. DEEMER opens front door, and he and JANNIE begin putting things like kerosene cans and produce out front for display. JANNIE chatters.*)

Robb organised a football sleepover at the gym last
night, it's something new. He's never done a sleepover.
Everybody was to bring sleeping bags and stuff. Robb
and the Coaching Staff and the boys, all sleeping there
on the gym floor. He didn't want the boys out getting
into trouble on Halloween.

DEEMER: They'll do it, too.

JANNIE: He likes to focus them on the game. If Robb had
his way, the boys wouldn't even go to class on a game day.

DEEMER: Coach knows his ball all right.

JANNIE: I told the girls that Daddy was at a slumber party
and they thought that was the funniest thing. We hardly
see Robb during football season. I think I probably made
sure the girls were born in July so Robb would have
time for their birthdays. It was the only thing I ever did
right. Except now Robb's talking about starting summer
practice even earlier, in July now, if he can get away
with it.

DEEMER: I'd say the county'd let Coach do anything he
wants he makes it to district. We never had a coach like
Coach before.

JANNIE: Really?

DEEMER: You know, somebody to win like he does. How
does Coach do it? He don't yell much. He thinks, don't he?

JANNIE: Robb likes making things right.

(*LEONA enters from the back with Halloween candy in cart. She
crosses to display. Sound effect of freight elevator ascending.*)

LEONA: Somebody's been in the ice machine back there.
Water all over the floor.

DEEMER: It was them kids.

JANNIE: Losing a little ice won't hurt us. Leona, what time
are you taking lunch?

LEONA: Whenever.

JANNIE: Anytime's fine. I need to make up a lunch
schedule. I've got it on my list.

LEONA: I don't eat, my sugar acts up. Mine's not as bad as my momma's and her smoking so much, too. Dr Guanzo says she'll lose her leg, half the time it's so swole up it turns black.

JANNIE: How about eleven thirty?

LEONA: That's early for me.

JANNIE: Twelve then. What about you, Deemer?

LEONA: Him and Claude switch off.

DEEMER: 'Cept yesterday one of them old drunks sits by the post office dropped dead and me and Claude went together over to see.

JANNIE: And a customer wanted twenty bags of winter feed and neither Leona or me could work the freight elevator.

DEEMER: There's a trick to it.

LEONA: And it ain't one I'm learning.

DEEMER: Me and Claude are the onliest ones know it, but I can show you.

JANNIE: It should be fixed. I'll put it on my list.

DEEMER: Mrs Lambert, I wouldn't get no elevator man here if I was you.

JANNIE: Why not?

LEONA: Because it's unfit, that's why not.

DEEMER: Last time, oh, about four years back, inspector come and shut it down, but I think he forgot about it because he never come back.

JANNIE: Deemer, you take eleven thirty and tell Claude he's got twelve thirty.

(*Sound effect of a truck horn from back.*)

DEEMER: That driver back from Doc's wants his money.

JANNIE: I'll go talk to him.

(*JANNIE exits to back. DEEMER gets out his sign making things. Sound effect of freight elevator descending. CLAUDE enters from elevator with dolly full of horse and mule feed.*)

DEEMER: Claude, spell me Halloween.

LEONA: It's right in front of you.

DEEMER: I can't read and write the same time. H–

CLAUDE: H–A–L–L–O–W–E–E–N.

DEEMER: Slow down. H–A–L– Hey, Claude, she said to take your dinner break at twelve thirty.

LEONA: Calls it lunch.

DEEMER: I'll tell you when.

CLAUDE: When you tell me, I will know the exact moment. L–O–W.

DEEMER: L–O–W– Low. Hal-low.

CLAUDE: E–E–N.

DEEMER: Een. Halloween. That's a right big word. Spell dinosaur.

CLAUDE: D–I–N–O–S–A–U–R. He doesn't like her here.

DEEMER: What?

CLAUDE: The Coach. He doesn't like her here.

DEEMER: You think so.

CLAUDE: It makes him very angry.

LEONA: Gossip.

DEEMER: You hear that over to Doc's?

CLAUDE: No.

LEONA: I'll tell you what. It takes a man one whole year to get used to anything they didn't make the cause of.

DEEMER: How come?

LEONA: A man's a man, and he's born of woman. They all of them had mothers.

DEEMER: You got you a mother, Claude?

CLAUDE: Her name was Mom.

LEONA: Then it's a wife takes over to pave the way. Happens every time. How'm I to do anything with this clock sitting here.

DEEMER: Move it.

LEONA: I don't touch clocks. You know I don't. Time is of the Lord.

(*JANNIE enters from back.*)

JANNIE: Everything's fine. The driver's coming back by this afternoon, and I'll go home at lunch and get the checkbook.

DEEMER: You're lucky. It's that sorry driver, too.

LEONA: Him letting Claude pile all that feed front of the restroom door knowing full well.

JANNIE: The driver told me my predecessor here had a reputation for avoiding payment, or our credit would be better. (*Pause.*) Deemer, I asked Claude not to put any more feed out here.

DEEMER: That's enough, Claude.

(*CLAUDE finishes unloading. He exits to back.*)

JANNIE: Is Claude (*Pause.*) all right?

DEEMER: Looks fine to me. He hadden said nothin.

LEONA: She means in the head.

DEEMER: It depends. Claude can name you thirty-three different kinds of dinosaurs, and he's read every book there is in the library on dinosaurs.

JANNIE: Then he's not retarded.

LEONA: What a person is is his own business.

DEEMER: There's just some people he don't hear when they talk.

JANNIE: Like me. (*Pause.*) But he hears you and Leona. Why is that?

DEEMER: (*Pause.*) I don't want to say.

JANNIE: Deemer–

DEEMER: (*Pause.*) Claude says he don't listen to no liars.

JANNIE: Liars? Why does he think I'm a liar?

DEEMER: It's managers, too. We ain't never had us a manager here Claude'd listen to, neither.

JANNIE: (*Pause.*) Well, one thing I can't allow is Claude shooting pigeons on the roof during business hours.

DEEMER: We got a bad problem with pigeons. Getting in the feed upstairs. They come through the windows and the walls.

LEONA: Bad as rats.

DEEMER: Worst. Their shit's bigger.

JANNIE: Maybe then on a Sunday, but not during the week. Deemer, tell Claude no more shooting upstairs.

DEEMER: Yes, mam.

(*The telephone rings. LEONA answers it.*)

LEONA: Co-op.

(*She hands the phone to JANNIE.*)

JANNIE: Jannie Lambert. (*Pause.*) Hi, Ted. (*Long pause.*) Wasn't he at the sleepover? The *sleepover*– At the gym last night? The football sleepover? I thought– Robb said– I'm sure there's a good reason. Sure. I know you were worried. Maybe he had a flat tire or– Sure. I'll call you. Bye-bye.

(*JANNIE hangs up the telephone. For a few moments the co-op is dead still. DEEMER works on his sign. LEONA adjusts hairpins. JANNIE is frozen. Sound effect of freight elevator ascending.*)

DEEMER: Sure is dead.

LEONA: K-Mart's got a big sale on. Circular in yesterday's paper.

DEEMER: Social security checks don't come in til Monday. Things is slow all over. What with coal being what it is and nobody much botherin to farm.

LEONA: It's the union killed coal.

DEEMER: No point farming when a patch of tobacco don't even pay. You hear what tobacco's down to?

LEONA: A man's work is the will of God, and there the coal union sits thinking they can legislate the will of God.

DEEMER: (*To JANNIE.*) What do you want this candy sign say exactly?

JANNIE: What?

DEEMER: 'Bout the Halloween candy.

JANNIE: Oh, uh, four bags for a dollar. No, five bags for a dollar. I think I'll mark the horse wormer kits that came in. Where's the marker, Leona?

LEONA: It's broke.

DEEMER: You put a new marker on your list two days ago.

JANNIE: That's right. (*Pause.*) Do you have a date for the football game tonight, Deemer?

DEEMER: No, mam. Not me, not women.

JANNIE: You all go to the games, Leona?

LEONA: Friday nights we go up to the skate rink to Christian Family Skate Night.

DEEMER: Leona says football's a sin.

LEONA: Senseless idolatry.

DEEMER: Leona's tabernacle. They don't sanction no organisations but the church and the roller rink.

LEONA: Rink does a fair business of a Friday night, playing gospel music and every half hour they do a mystery Bible verse for the kids over the PA. All of us goes, course not momma and my husband's lungs can't take no physical activity and Leandra's got her club foot.

(*A customer enters from front door. FATHER is a black Roman Catholic priest from Africa.*)

FATHER: I see someone wants to play tricks against you—

JANNIE: Father!

FATHER: Greetings! (*To LEONA.*) I bring you glad tidings of nice clean crisp bank money.

JANNIE: Leona and I have had a talk about that.

FATHER: About our bingo money? I think it's admirable, completely admirable. It is refreshing to find this sort of conviction lurking around today. Are you Pentecostal, Leona?

DEEMER: Tabernacle.

LEONA: Over in the valley, The Bible Church of Jesus's True and Only Name.

FATHER: Ah. Which is?

LEONA: What?

FATHER: Jesus true and only name?

LEONA: Jesus.

FATHER: Oh, I see. Yes.

JANNIE: Father, we have coffee today. I brought a coffee maker in. Would you like some?

FATHER: Yes, very much, please. I have been at Doc's picking up the gossip, but I cannot drink Doc's coffee. We disagree.

(*JANNIE exits to office.*)

DEEMER: Ain't nobody Doc's coffee agrees with. You lay any money down?

FATHER: Of course.

DEEMER: On Coach?

FATHER: Absolutely. Twenty on our Tigers. And if I win, Leona, I'll give it back henceforth it came. Besides the game, quite the thing at Doc's this morning was the Halloween hijinx... your theft, that dog in the coffin and the hairdresser, what is her name, the large one?

LEONA: Wanda. She's at the tabernacle with me.

FATHER: Miss Wanda reported a man lurking in the alleyway outside her shop last night.

LEONA: She does her perms on a Thursday night.

FATHER: She said the man carried a rifle sort of gun and shook it at her.

DEEMER: I'd say it weren't but a deerhunter going to the video store.

(*JANNIE enters from office with coffee for herself and FATHER.*)

FATHER: With rifle in hand in case a deer should bound wildly out of Wanda's Beauty Salon?

JANNIE: We have sugar but no cream. The milkman hasn't come yet.

LEONA: And won't neither 'til he gets paid.

JANNIE: Is it deer season already?

FATHER: Apparently. Every car and truck out there has a large dead animal tied to the roof. Does Robb hunt?

JANNIE: No, thank God. Losing a husband to football is bad enough.

FATHER: What does he do with all those guns?

JANNIE: Did Robb show you his guns? Here, Leona, run this over to the bank and get us some change, too.

(*LEONA takes the deposit bag from JANNIE.*)

LEONA: (*To FATHER.*) Are you all grape juice or wine?

FATHER: Our Lord said it was His Blood, therefore we drink His Blood.

LEONA: Blood!

(*LEONA exits out front door to bank.*)

JANNIE: Robb's guns are an investment. They're all special edition guns, you know, to collect, with little histories about them and plaques...

FATHER: Investment guns. I had no idea.

JANNIE: Robb wants the right kind of display case for them in the living room with lights in it, but it costs a fortune. The guns cost a fortune.

DEEMER: (*To FATHER.*) You drink real blood?

FATHER: Yes.

JANNIE: No, we don't. Go, check our shell stock, Deemer.

(*DEEMER crosses to check shelf.*)

(*To FATHER.*) Now it will be all over town that we drink blood. We'll be right in there with the snake churches.

FATHER: It's amazing the way the superstitions about the Roman Church pervade your American backwaters.

JANNIE: They think we're voodoo.

FATHER: Why not? With an African priest and a parish full of Filipino doctors.

DEEMER: Mrs Lambert–

FATHER: But they love our bingo on Wednesday nights.

DEEMER: Mrs Lambert– It was ammo they was after. They cleaned us out.

JANNIE: Where?

(*JANNIE follows DEEMER to see the empty shelf.*)

DEEMER: Not a box left.

JANNIE: The police didn't see this?

DEEMER: Diddent look.

FATHER: Frank was still over at Doc's when I left.

JANNIE: Deemer, run over and get him.

(*DEEMER exits out front door.*)

God, I swear game days are always like this. What ever can go wrong usually does.

FATHER: Except the game.

JANNIE: Except the game.

FATHER: I don't know much about American football. I once followed the Chicago Bears.

JANNIE: Robb's teams always win.

FATHER: That must be nice. I certainly know everyone is glad to have him here. (*Pause.*) Robb wasn't with you and the girls trick or treating last night.

JANNIE: (*Pause.*) He was with the team. (*Pause.*) They had a sleepover at the gym last night.

FATHER: Did the girls like their bookmarkers?

JANNIE: What?

FATHER: I had to give them some old bookmarkers I had from Lourdes. I wish I had had candy, but I've never had trick or treaters before.

JANNIE: They were fine.

FATHER: Did you see them? They had 3-D photos of dying pilgrims being lowered into the holy waters. Children love things like that. It's been such a joy for me to have you and your family here, Jan. You're the real thing.

JANNIE: It's that good old parochial school training.

FATHER: I can see how familiar you and Robb are at mass – as if you were brushing your teeth.

JANNIE: Is that good?

FATHER: I think it is exactly how our Lord intended it. We are such a small and heathen outpost here in the mountains.

JANNIE: Don't you get lonely?

FATHER: Loneliness is a gift from God.

JANNIE: But, I mean, there not being any other black people–

FATHER: Oh, no, I was much hungrier for good fellow Romans.

JANNIE: The Filipino doctors seem pretty nice. A bunch of them gave Robb a new van for the football team to use.

FATHER: Do you know why there are no black people here? In the twenties, they lynched four black men for stealing sheep, and the entire black community moved to Castlewood. Doc, Frank, Deemer – they've all told me the story.

JANNIE: That's horrible. Then why would they have sent you here?

FATHER: For the transfiguration. Do you believe in answered prayers, Jannie?

JANNIE: I don't know.

FATHER: Of course you do. We all, believers and unbelievers, ask hoping to receive. Our Lord went to the mountains, praying, asking for who knows what, and he ended up talking to Elijah and Moses and glowing like a Halloween jack-o-lantern. What kind of answer was that, I wonder. (*Pause.*) I seriously doubt the Bishop knew he was answering my prayers by sending me here. He apologised for days. (*Pause.*) I have this weakness. For little black boys. Fortunately Filipino or white won't do in my case, so you see this is the perfect place for me to be. I prayed for deliverance, and I ended up here in the mountains. We ask for card tricks, and God gives us cataclysms. (*Pause.*) I've shocked you. I'm sorry.

JANNIE: No–

FATHER: I made you my confessor.

JANNIE: It must be hard not to– I mean, everyone coming to you, and you not having someone to, I mean...

FATHER: Why are you here? Did you and Robb come for the transfiguration, too?

JANNIE: Just Robb's job.

FATHER: I wouldn't think this was the kind of place for a winner.

JANNIE: We won't be here that long. Maybe another year. We average about two years with a team, then we move.

FATHER: Every two years?

JANNIE: Robb likes fixing bad teams. He'll take the team apart and rebuild it and they win and we move. I'm used to it.

FATHER: Are you? I hate being a nomad. I've done it always.

JANNIE: It's just the way Robb is.

FATHER: There you go.

JANNIE: And every small town is the same, pretty much. After a while.

(*Sound effect of freight elevator descending. CLAUDE enters with dolly full of horse and mule feed bags.*)

Damn it, Claude! I told you, I told you! Take it all upstairs!

(*CLAUDE crosses to other unloaded bags and begins unloading.*)

He won't listen to me. I can't stop him.

FATHER: Claude, Mrs Lambert doesn't want the feed in here. She wants it upstairs.

(*CLAUDE stops unloading.*)

(*To CLAUDE.*) What are you building?

CLAUDE: Something.

(*CLAUDE exits into elevator. Sound effect of elevator ascending.*)

FATHER: (*Laughing.*) He's determined to build you something.

JANNIE: I can't do this. Robb's right. I can't do this. It's all a mess! None of it works right. Robb was right.

(*JANNIE crosses and takes a bandanna off the shelf to wipe her eyes. Then laughs.*) Deemer says Claude doesn't hear what liars say.

FATHER: There's nothing worse than a righteous idiot. Are you all right?

JANNIE: I'm fine. I am. Really.

FATHER: Are you sure?

JANNIE: Yes.

FATHER: It's not Claude, is it.

JANNIE: Robb hasn't shown up at school this morning. They're holding up the pep rally until he gets there. One of the assistant coaches called me.

FATHER: Do you know where Robb is?

JANNIE: It's a game day. Robb wouldn't miss the pep rally.

FATHER: But he was at the sleepover—

JANNIE: There wasn't a sleepover last night.

FATHER: You haven't seen him since yesterday, then—

JANNIE: One time, when Robb was first coaching, we were in North Carolina, and we couldn't find Robb, and then he just showed up at the field before the game. He'd been at a motel, he said, clearing his brain.

FATHER: I can check the motel, Jannie.

JANNIE: No! Wherever Robb is, he's OK, and they'll win tonight like they always do. I'm sure he's fine.

(*Sound effect of elevator descending. CLAUDE enters with more horse and mule feed. He unloads the sacks in the same place. JANNIE is resigned.*)

FATHER: (*Pause.*) Are you a saint, Claude?

CLAUDE: A saint?

FATHER: Known or unknown?

CLAUDE: Unknown.

FATHER: Myself, as well. Today is the feast day of All Saints, but tomorrow is our day, Claude, the democratic day of All Souls.

JANNIE: Will you say a Mass for the Dead?

FATHER: At least three. Our Filipino doctors are quite particular about their Masses for the Dead. I may even use my Latin if you promise not to turn me in.

CLAUDE: Latin is a dead language.

FATHER: Which I think would be appropriate, don't you think?

CLAUDE: yes.

(*CLAUDE exits to back. DEEMER enters from front door.*)

DEEMER: Police's coming, but he needs to go talk to Wanda first.

JANNIE: Deemer, I don't want any more horse and mule feed in here. You must make Claude understand.

DEEMER: Sure. Hey, Claude–

(*DEEMER exits to back.*)

JANNIE: Everything will be all right.

FATHER: (*Pause.*) I'm going to tell you something that you may not understand nor believe, but you must listen. This is the edge of the world, Jan, these mountains we've come to. If we wait here, something will come and push us over. We're too close to the edge. (*Pause.*) I've come here to the edge of everything because there is no place left for me to go. But you, on the other hand–

(*LEONA enters from front door.*)

LEONA: Bank said they're going to have to start charging us for any more overdrafts.

JANNIE: I'll take care of it.

LEONA: You better tell the Board of Directors, I'd say.

JANNIE: I will take care of it, Leona.

(*DEEMER enters from back.*)

As long as we're not working, let's play. Deemer, get some butcher paper. We're going to make a sign for the Tigers. Go, Tigers Go! Across the front window!

(*DEEMER gets his paper and markers.*)

DEEMER: You want me to draw a tiger on it?

JANNIE: Of course I do.

FATHER: 'Tyger, tyger burning bright,
   In the forest of the night;
   What immortal hand or eye,
   Could frame thy fearful symmetry?'

JANNIE: Vanquish the Vikings!

DEEMER: I'd say we got it made tonight, they don't stick us with that old blind-eyed ref.

FATHER: Believe it or not, there was a purpose in my visit. I came to buy a rat trap. The little devils have been in the Host of all things.

DEEMER: I got just the thing. Look up on the counter, there.

   (*FATHER picks up the dead mice box.*)

   I got me ten of them suckers in one night.

FATHER: (*Reading.*) RoDo-DeMo.

DEEMER: See, they come in that hole to get the stuff that smells like cheese–

JANNIE: There are dead mice in that box?

DEEMER: And their guts explode.

LEONA: It's the best thing we ever tried that worked.

JANNIE: Go put it in the dumpster.

DEEMER: It ain't full yet. I got to put it back out tonight.

JANNIE: It's disgusting. I don't want to look at it.

DEEMER: Yes, mam.

   (*DEEMER exits to back with dead mice box. LEONA pokes JANNIE's clutter aside to clear space on the counter.*)

FATHER: You will forgive me if I buy two.

JANNIE: You should get a cat.

FATHER: Is that a kinder form of annihilation? Well, I must be off to meet the people in their proverbial streets as it were.

LEONA: Ten eleven.

FATHER: Out of a clean twenty, untainted by bingo.

(*DEEMER enters from back.*)

Don't worry, Deemer. We all should be martyrs for our enthusiasms.

DEEMER: That's OK.

FATHER: (*To JANNIE.*) I will do what I can. (*Pause.*) Oh, and according to Pope John Paul, All Saint's is your day today. He tells us to revere our young wives and mothers as the true saints of our age, which is a terrific burden for you all, actually. Chiao!

(*FATHER exits out of front door, first holding it open for JAM JAR LADY to enter.*)

JAM JAR LADY: You got canning jars?

DEEMER: You wanted slop buckets before.

JAM JAR LADY: I done changed my mind, smarty.

DEEMER: Jelly, wide-mouth, and quart, last aisle back.

(*JAM JAR LADY shops in the store.*)

He's like your preacher, idden he?

LEONA: Calling bingo of a Wednesday night.

JANNIE: How do you know? Were you there?

LEONA: I know.

DEEMER: He come from Africa, Doc said.

LEONA: You blame him?

JANNIE: He is a priest. And he was educated at Cambridge. In England. In Europe. And we are very lucky to have him here.

DEEMER: He talks good.

LEONA: All preachers talk good. They been given the gift what makes them preachers.

(*DEEMER holds up the football sign.*)

JANNIE: (*Reading it.*) Varnish the Vikings. Close enough.

DEEMER: This is the Tiger, here, and them here's Vikings lying dead around and a Viking in his mouth. Where do you want it?

JANNIE: Across the window. There–

(*DEEMER moves the ladder against the high window overlooking the street.*)

DEEMER: Hey, Leona, get me some tape.

LEONA: In a minute. I got something stuck in my tooth.

(*Picking at her tooth, LEONA exits to office to get tape. A Filipino Doctor's wife, MRS GUANZO, enters from the front door. She is expensively dressed and carries a Louis Vuitton handbag and a piece of paper in her hand.*)

JANNIE: (*To MRS GUANZO.*) Good morning.

DEEMER: That's Dr Guanzo's wife. She don't know no English.

(*JANNIE takes the paper from her.*)

JANNIE: (*Reading.*) Bird seed.

DEEMER: We don't have none. Give her scratch.

JANNIE: Are you sure?

DEEMER: Chickens is birds and chickens eat scratch.

(*JANNIE exits to back to get scratch, LEONA enters, from office with tape.*)

LEONA: Hiddee-do, Mrs Guanzo.

(*MRS GUANZO smiles.*)

DEEMER: She only speaks Philipines.

LEONA: I know her. Dr Guanzo's the one wants to take Momma's leg. He's been real nice about it. What'd she come after?

(*Sound effect of a gunshot outside in the street. JANNIE enters from back with a bag full of chicken scratch. MRS GUANZO laughs and indicates it's way too much.*)

DEEMER: Bird seed.

LEONA: (*To JANNIE.*) She dudn't want that whole thing.

JANNIE: (*Struggling with the bag.*) Thank you Leona.

(*Sound effect of a gunshot, outside.*)

Is that a gun?

(*JANNIE opens the scratch to measure out less. JAMJAR LADY crosses to check out with a case of jam jars.*)

(*To JAMJAR LADY.*) Were you finding everything you needed?

JAM JAR LADY: My legs hold out, I'm gonna make me some crab apple jelly. I saved them crab apples on a count of being my old man's favourite, but I ain't had my legs to speak of, and if them apples ain't rotted on me, now.

LEONA: (*Ringing JAM JAR LADY up.*) I know what you mean. My momma's bout to lose her good leg. Six ninety eight and tax makes seven twelve.

JANNIE: Mrs Guanzo, about a pound, you think. A pound?

(*MRS GUANZO smiles and nods.*)

LEONA: Pretty little thing, idn't she?

DEEMER: (*To JAM JAR LADY.*) Need any help with that, mam?

JAM JAR LADY: Ain't nothing wrong with my arms, Praise Jesus.

(*Sound effect of a gunshot.*)

JANNIE: Is that Claude shooting? Deemer, go tell him to stop this minute!

(*JAM JAR LADY exits out of front door. DEEMER starts to exit to freight elevator, but CLAUDE enters from back. JANNIE sees CLAUDE as more gunshots sound outside. Sound effects offstage: JAM JAR LADY screams and the sound of a box of jam jars hitting the pavement.*)

It's not Claude! What is it! What's happening?!

(*Sound effect of another gunshot. LEONA panics and drops behind checkout counter to hide. JANNIE moves like a sleepwalker. DEEMER runs to the ladder and climbs it to see what's happening outside. CLAUDE crosses to the front door, calmly like a curious child, hiding behind the bunker of feed sacks he has made. MRS GUANZO smiles bravely but is confused.*)

DEEMER: Bullseye! You see that, Claude! Buddy, and he's hitting 'em, too. That's Shiftlet, president of the bank, looks like. See them bodies, Claude, over to the bank parking lot? And that lady that was in here after jam jars.

(*Sound effect of a gunshot.*)

JANNIE: Deemer, get down! Get Claude back!

DEEMER: Here come the police. 'Cept they oughtn't better park there.

(*Sound effect of a gunshot.*)

Yes, he did, too. Got him a cop. Can't see which one. Hey, Claude was that Frank or his brother?

CLAUDE: His brother.

LEONA: (*To MRS GUANZO.*) Honey, there's somebody gone crazy out there shooting people! Get over here!

JANNIE: It sounds like it's coming from upstairs.

CLAUDE: He is upstairs.

DEEMER: From the way the dead's laying, I'd say he's on our side of the street.

CLAUDE: He is upstairs.

JANNIE: What?

DEEMER: The cops pulled over behind the funeral home.

JANNIE: Claude, what did you say?

LEONA: I hope everybody in this room knows the only true name of Jesus and personally calls him Lord and Saviour Almighty and Master, Amen.

JANNIE: Claude! Deemer, ask him! Claude, is the person who's shooting upstairs in this building? Deemer?

DEEMER: You seen somebody, Claude?

CLAUDE: Many times. We spoke.

JANNIE: I need to call the police and tell them this person is upstairs.

(*Sound effect of a gunshot.*)

DEEMER: Talk about stupid. Wanda run out of the beauty shop and didn't get more than two feet; 'course she's 'bout the biggest target in town.

MRS GUANZO: Jesu Maria Joseph! Anang nangyari! (What's happening!)

LEONA: Stay with us, Jesus.

JANNIE: I've got to call the police.

(*JANNIE looks up phone number, then dials.*)

LEONA: Mightier than all lightening, fire of fires, swing thou mighty sword, Jehovah! Smite thou evil, gore thou death, impale the fallen angel!

MRS GUANZO: Ay naku, diyos ko! (Oh, my God)

JANNIE: I can't hear. Hello?

LEONA: (*To MRS GUANZO.*) Kneel with me, honey. Here. Bring us righteous devastation and wrap us in tongues of fire, O Lord, and–

JANNIE: I can't hear! Hello! This is Jannie Lambert down at the farm co-op. (*Pause.*) Yes, it is exciting–

(*Sound effect of a gunshot.*)

DEEMER: That was Cooter!

JANNIE: –that person who's shooting is upstairs here we think and I wondered–

CLAUDE: Cooter–

JANNIE: –I wondered what we should do. Hello?

DEEMER: See him there lying in the middle of the road.

JANNIE: Oh, Thank God, you're there–

LEONA: Cooter who?

DEEMER: That old town dog walks around. Old Cooter won't be peeing on my bicycle no more.

JANNIE: Yes, tell them he's here, upstairs. No, we don't know who it is–

(*JANNIE hangs up the phone.*)

She's going to have a policeman call us and tell us what to do. It's going to be all right.

DEEMER: I can see 'em standing over behind the funeral parlor talking with their two-ways.

JANNIE: We'll just have to sit tight.

LEONA: You better be kneeling.

(*Sound effect of a gunshot.*)

DEEMER: 'Bout time he missed. (*Pause.*) There some cops sneaking up the alley by the video store. (*Pause.*) Looks like they're motioning for us to try and make it over there.

JANNIE: Really? Where?

LEONA: I ain't going nowhere.

JANNIE: Could we make it?

DEEMER: Edging down our side, staying close in, 'til we get there opposite, I'd say we might could.

JANNIE: (*To DEEMER.*) You want to try?

DEEMER: Uh, no, mam.

JANNIE: (*Pause.*) I'm going. (*Pause.*) Deemer, you and Claude block off the way to the back. There's no other way in here from up stairs.

DEEMER: Lest he's a genius with elevators.

JANNIE: Could he?

DEEMER: Not lest he knows the right place to kick.

JANNIE: Open the elevator door so he can't call it up. Just in case. Now, listen. I'm going out there and I'll tell the police he's upstairs an that he can't get to you all, and they'll figure something out.

(*JANNIE moves to front door.*)

I can't think about it.

(*She breathes deeply.*)

I have to just do it.

(*She makes the sign of the cross and exits from front door, edging along outer wall out of sight. CLAUDE barricades the doors to the back. He doesn't open up the elevator door. DEEMER crosses to ladder and climbs it to watch.*)

DEEMER: Hey, Leona, you think it could be old Tottie Crabtree up there?

LEONA: Tottie?

DEEMER: After all that trouble to the bank?

LEONA: (*To MRS GUANZO.*) I bet you know Tottie Crabtree. Dr Guanzo put that plastic hip joint in for him.

MRS GUANZO: Tautree Crabtree?

CLAUDE: It isn't Tottie.

LEONA: What's she doing? Can you see her?

DEEMER: Not yet.

LEONA: Tottie don't know her real good, and he might shoot her by mistake.

DEEMER: (*Excitedly.*) She's got it! Yes, sir, the cops is motioning for her to come on. She's got it.

LEONA: Did she make it?

DEEMER: She's stopped. In the middle of the street, just standing there looking up.

LEONA: Let me see.

DEEMER: Like she was blinded.

CLAUDE: She saw him.

DEEMER: She turned around. She's coming on back.

LEONA: It's the truth. All I ever said about her is the honest naked truth.

(*JANNIE enters from front door, ashen and shaken.*)

DEEMER: You had it, too.

LEONA: She's fainting! Get her a pop, Claude.

(*LEONA settles JANNIE down on the feed sacks. CLAUDE crosses to cooler.*)

DEEMER: Tottie must of thought it weren't much game you standing there still like that.

LEONA: (*To CLAUDE.*) And get her a 7-Up! You don't give Coke for somebody fainting.

(*Sound effect of a gunshot. JANNIE jumps as if hit.*)

DEEMER: Tottie got him a trooper that time. (*DEEMER lets CLAUDE out of the cooler.*)

LEONA: (*To JANNIE.*) Honey, did you see him?

DEEMER: I'd say that's what froze her up.

LEONA: He was afraid Tottie might not know you, you being new here.

DEEMER: We done guessed who's shooting upstairs.

JANNIE: No! Don't–

DEEMER: You know old Tottie Crabtree wears that hat? Claude, you know Tottie could shoot like that?

JANNIE: (*Pause.*) Tottie Crabtree?

DEEMER: Instead of him making his payment on the farm last month, Old Tottie took him a shotgun down to the bank, and said they wouldn't bleed another penny out of him.

LEONA: 'Course they'd given over the Christmas Club money to Tottie's wife after she'd left him for that coal miner man and Tottie'd been the one putting the money in all year regular.

DEEMER: Tottie and Mr Shiftlet over to the bank's all the time having words. And Mr Shiftlet's lying there shot in the bank parking lot.

JANNIE: And you think it's Tottie Crabtree upstairs?

LEONA: But Tottie never give us a bit of trouble.

CLAUDE: It isn't Tottie.

LEONA: Tottie always pays regular on his credit here.

(*Sound effect of a gunshot. Pause. Second gunshot.*)

DEEMER: Took him two shots, but he got hisself a dark looking man over in the bank parking lot again.

LEONA: Claude, get up there and take Tottie's gun away from him this minute.

JANNIE: No!

LEONA: Go on, Claude.

(*CLAUDE doesn't move.*)

You old big thing, don't tell me you're afraid of Tottie Crabtree. You'd make five of him.

DEEMER: A gun kind of evens things out.

LEONA: I'll go up. I'm not afraid of Tottie Crabtree.

JANNIE: No one is going up there.

LEONA: Well, then, call you the police and tell them it's Tottie Crabtree upstairs and they'll all split a gut laughing.

DEEMER: Here comes the Bread Man.

LEONA: The Bread Man.

JANNIE: The Bread Man?! How could he have gotten through? Don't the police have barricades up?

DEEMER: Nope. They're yelling to him from over at Doc's.

(*Sound effect of a gunshot. BREAD MAN enters from front door with racks of bread.*)

BREAD MAN: Hidey-do. Twenty whites, two brown, a rye and a birthday cake.

DEEMER: I'd say today is your lucky day. Lady side of your bread truck just got her nose shot in.

LEONA: Tottie Crabtree's upstairs shooting people.

BREAD MAN: Hey, Mrs Guanzo. How's the Doctor? (*To LEONA.*) I brung them coffee cakes and fried pies you asked me for, and we got a special on crumb cakes.

(*Sound effect of a gunshot.*)

DEEMER: Look out. Lady got it in the boomerangs.

BREAD MAN: Pardon?

DEEMER: Lady painted on your truck.

BREAD MAN: We got a special on crumb cakes on through next Wednesday.

LEONA: They do good.

BREAD MAN: Pardon?

LEONA: I said they do good.

BREAD MAN: I'm 'bout deaf of these sinuses, all up in here, swoll all up, here where it's red. And it's run to my ears and I can't hear a blessed thing.

(*Outside, sound effect of more gunshots. BREAD MAN shelves bread.*)

LEONA: That wudn't right Mr Shiftlet handing Tottie's Christmas Club money over to his wife like that, and there's a penalty too for you taking it out before December one.

(*Sound effect of a gunshot.*)

BREAD MAN: You all want those crumb cakes?

LEONA: They do real good.

BREAD MAN: Pardon?

LEONA: They do real good, but she's the manager.

JANNIE: (*To BREAD MAN.*) Don't go back out there.

BREAD MAN: Pardon?

JANNIE: Deemer, stop him! Please!

BREAD MAN: Lady, I got to be to Safeway by ten past. Crumb cakes or no crumb cakes?

LEONA: Crumb cakes.

BREAD MAN: Pardon?

LEONA: Crumb cakes.

(*BREAD MAN exits. Sound effect of a gunshot.*)

CLAUDE: No crumb cakes.

JANNIE: Oh, my God.

LEONA: Sweet Jesus, I'll tell you what's the truth. Tottie is bad upset.

FATHER: (*Offstage. His voice is amplified from the street.*) Hello! Up there, can you hear me? I think you can. I know you can see me, and I am acting on faith. I am trusting you. You have done what you came to do, now, please, lay down your weapons and surrender peacefully. No one will hurt you. You have my word. If you want, I will escort you personally to the police van. I will shield you with my own body. You have my word. (*Pause.*) You have family, maybe or children? Please think of them and their forgiveness. (*Pause.*) You have vented your anger. You are at peace now. I can feel it. I know. Come down and I will walk with you.

(*Pause. Silence. Sound effect of a gunshot.*)

DEEMER: Somebody ain't learning too fast.

JANNIE: (*In a whisper.*) That was Father.

DEEMER: I don't guess that bullet-proof stuff works too good like on TV. That old boy is deader than a Christmas battery in June. (*Pause.*) Hey, Claude, lookee there.

(*Sound effect of a helicopter.*)

JANNIE: A helicopter?

DEEMER: It's a National Guard's, aint it Claude? Sure is.

MRS GUANZO: Santa Maria, Ina ng pañginoon!–

LEONA: (*To MRS GUANZO.*) Hold on, honey, they're coming to get us.

MRS GUANZO: –Ipagdarasal mo kaming makasalaman, sa ngayon–

(*Deafening sound of low flying helicopter. Sound effect of elevator ascending. Shotlike sounds, then, in a few places, raggedy puffs of smoke filter down from upstairs. MRS GUANZO cries out the Hail, Mary.*)

JANNIE: Are we on fire?

MRS GUANZO: –at sa horas ng aming kamataya–

CLAUDE: Tear gas.

JANNIE: Are you sure?

(*Through the front door, a man in riot gear falls. JANNIE runs to his side and pulls the helmet from his face. It is FATHER.*)

JANNIE: Father.

(*Pause. Breathless.*)

FATHER: I found him.

JANNIE: Father, I don't know what to do. Help me, please!

FATHER: (*Dying.*) "Save me, O God; for the waters are coming into my soul–"

(*Sound effect of a gunshot. More smoke coming down. Everyone coughing.*)

"–I sink in deep mire, where there is no standing, I am–"

JANNIE: Tell me what to do.

FATHER: "–weary of my crying (*Pause.*) – shame covers my face. I am–"

LEONA: I've had about enough. I'm going up there.

FATHER: "–my shame–"

JANNIE: Leona, no.

(*JANNIE struggles with LEONA. MRS GUANZO crouches beside FATHER.*)

Help me, Claude. She can't go up there.

(*CLAUDE doesn't help.*)

FATHER: "–vinegar to drink (*Pause.*) –vinegar–"

MRS GUANZO: Uh! Paya na Siya! (Oh, he's dead!)

> (*FATHER dies. MRS GUANZO takes off her jacket and covers his face. She crosses herself. Sound effect of a helicopter as it swoops low and retreats. It's sound wanes into the sound of the descending freight elevator. Everyone is still suddenly. MRS GUANZO bolts, exiting out of front door.*)

LEONA: No, honey, don't–

> (*The elevator doors open. A man dressed in "Tiger" sweats and athletic shoes. He carries an IGLOO beer cooler, a rifle, and a cartridge belt.*)

DEEMER: Hey, Coach.

> (*JANNIE turns slowly to look at her husband. Blackout.*)
> (*End of Act One.*)

ACT TWO

Co-op interior. A few seconds later.

ROBB: (*Laughing.*) Whoa! Dragging out the damn National Guard helicopter. I never thought that old bathtub could fly. (*Pause.*) Tell me those old boys out there aren't loving every damn minute of this.

(*ROBB sets the beer cooler down.*)

Shooo. What in the hell is that stuff, Big Claude? Laughing Gas? Is that what you all do over at the armory, sit around sniffing laughing gas? That stuff'd make a skunk leave the country. God, I'm hungry. Anything here to eat that hasn't been sitting on the shelf 200 years?

(*Pause. No-one answers him.*)

Eat. You put it between your teeth and chew.

DEEMER: We got some cakes, but no crumb cakes; and some nabs.

ROBB: What kind?

DEEMER: Peanut butter, cheese on rye, cheese on ritz, cheese on whole wheat.

ROBB: Cheese on wheat. Jannie likes me to eat my whole grains.

(*DEEMER hands ROBB a couple packages of nabs.*)

Ice me down a six pack, Deemer, and we'll be in business. Here, wait a minute, let's dump these empties.

DEEMER: You like them longneck returnables, don't you, Coach?

ROBB: Damn right. Great! (*DEEMER enters cooler with beer cooler. ROBB eats cracker.*) I don't believe it. It's not too stale. Oh, by the way, Shiftlet didn't give me the loan for the camper. (*To JANNIE.*) Did you hear what I said? We're talking, what? A nothing loan. Nothin at all, and he turns me down. So I gave Shiftlet a new lease on life.

LEONA: You're drunk.

ROBB: I hope so. Let's find out. Put an apple on her head, Big Claude. If I hit it she's wrong. If I miss it, she's right.

(*CLAUDE hands ROBB an apple. He takes a bite out of it then sticks it on LEONA's head. It is held in position by the rigidity of her hairdo.*)

LEONA: Son of God, save us from this sinner.

ROBB: You could carry a whole damn fruit basket up here, you know that? Leona, gunfire is a very sobering thing. It snaps your brain open and shut like a coin purse. Ready?

JANNIE: Robb–

ROBB: Don't worry. It's all right. This is a John Wayne Memorial Winchester. Look at the carving on the butt of this baby, Claude. It's called "The Duke".

(*LEONA takes the apple off her head.*)

LEONA: He's coo-coo. You should of told somebody!

ROBB: She's right, Jannie. You really should have told somebody.

LEONA: Out of your own home and family.

ROBB: It is embarrassing, I know.

LEONA: And somebody said they was 'bout to make you Marshall of the Christmas parade!

ROBB: I'd say that's off. (*Pause.*) You know what I was going to say when I came in? "Honey, I'm home!" (*Laughs.*) Honey, I'm home. What was that damn movie? Do you remember? Some nutball killing people. You know. Jack Nicholson and that bad-assed grin of his? Jannie?

JANNIE: I can't remember.

ROBB: You didn't see half of it. She was down on the floor screaming her head off. (*Pause, eats his nab cracker.*) And Jesus, remember *Carrie*? The damn hand comes out of the ground, and Jannie kicks this old boy sitting in front of us in the head. Damn knee jerk reaction while she's screaming her head off.

JANNIE: You know I don't like scary movies.

ROBB: Won't even look. Will not look. I bet Big Claude likes scary movies.

CLAUDE: Sometimes.

(*CLAUDE has a bag of walnuts. He cracks them and eats them.*)

ROBB: We used to go to a lot of movies. Where was that? Where were we living when we used to go to all those movies?

JANNIE: Pennsylvania.

ROBB: It was some place civilised. Not like this.

JANNIE: It was in Pennsylvania.

ROBB: I'll think of it in a minute. (*Pause.*) It was before the kids. And they had dog races on Sunday. Our priest went to the damn dog races on Sunday.

(*DEEMER knocks to be let out of the cooler. ROBB crosses to cooler door, opens it. DEEMER enters with a bottle of beer in his hand. He hands it to ROBB.*)

Thanks, ace. What's it like out there, Claude?

CLAUDE: Fine.

ROBB: Are they working on any reinforcements?

CLAUDE: Two more trooper cars. (*Offers walnut.*) Want one?

ROBB: Sure. Crack it for me. (*To CLAUDE.*) You got my bunker built. It's looking good, Claude. We're in business. This is better than a damn game.

LEONA: (*To ROBB.*) They ain't gonna put up with this much longer! My husband had two good lungs working he'd show you what for and more, too.

ROBB: It's a joke out there. They're tripping all over themselves.

LEONA: Police know about people like you.

ROBB: They're scared shitless.

LEONA: They know you ain't nothing but crazy.

ROBB: Bristol Pistols! That's it. Bristol had two movie theaters right near us.

JANNIE: I don't think it was Bristol.

ROBB: It sure as hell was Bristol.

JANNIE: Molly was born in Bristol. We were living in the split-level.

LEONA: Tennessee or Virginia side?

JANNIE: Tennessee.

ROBB: Where's the church key, Deemer?

LEONA: Virginia side's better. Tennessee side you can buy whiskey in a grocery store.

ROBB: God, that was a game. Bristol, Virginia playing Bristol, Tennessee.

DEEMER: Yall win, Coach?

ROBB: Did we?

JANNIE: Not the first year. We lost every game.

ROBB: Damn.

DEEMER: But you fixed'm, didden you, Coach?

ROBB: I must have.

JANNIE: You did.

ROBB: I didn't think I'd ever get those cocksuckers playing ball.

DEEMER: Doc said you hadden ever lost a game.

JANNIE: He hasn't. Not since Bristol.

ROBB: Three years it took me getting that team right, Deemer. Jesus. I about gave up.

JANNIE: They gave us a new station wagon. They gave Robb a ten thousand dollar bonus, and one of the players' fathers flew us out to his beach house in Myrtle Beach...

ROBB: Yeah.

JANNIE: And we moved from Bristol to a trailer in Danville.

ROBB: Now that was a team. The Danville Dogs.

DEEMER: Why'd you leave Bristol, Coach?

ROBB: You got it, you got to spread it around.

DEEMER: Winning?

ROBB: I'm a fix-it man, Deemer.

DEEMER: How, Coach?

LEONA: Transacting with Satan.

ROBB: How'd you know, Leona?

JANNIE: The more you won, the more we lost.

ROBB: What?

JANNIE: Nothing.

ROBB: I said *what.*

JANNIE: I didn't say anything.

ROBB: Good. (*To DEEMER.*) I like knowing how things are
    going to turn out. You win, Deemer, you know how
    things are going to turn out. Go in on top, and leave on
    top. (*Pause.*) OK, everybody, lighten up. Help yourself to
    a beer, Deemer. Big Claude, you want a beer? Ladies?
    (*DEEMER enters cooler to get beer.*)

ROBB: (*To LEONA.*) God, you remind me of my mom,
    sniffing out your nose like that. Doesn't she, Jannie? (*To
    LEONA.*) Your hair's bigger, though. You towed the line
    with my mom, or buddy, you bailed out quick.

CLAUDE: Two more trooper cars.

ROBB: Everybody's got to feel important. Hell, this is the
    chance of a lifetime for these guys.

JANNIE: (*Pause.*) Where were you last night?

ROBB: Oh, yeah. The girls have fun? Did you get some
    pictures?

JANNIE: There wasn't a sleepover.

ROBB: It was Molly's first trick or treat, and Jannie made
    the girls the cutest damn costumes. What do you call
    them?

JANNIE: Raggedy Ann dolls.

ROBB: Yeah, and all this damn yarn hair. Took her a month
    just making the little wigs.

JANNIE: Ted called. There wasn't a sleepover.

ROBB: Sure there was. It was on the fifty yard line, and I was
    there.

LEONA: What do you want with us?

ROBB: What do you think I want with you?

LEONA: Let us go.

ROBB: Let you go.

(*DEEMER knocks from cooler to be let out. ROBB opens the door. DEEMER hands a beer to ROBB and CLAUDE and keeps one for himself.*)

LEONA: I got six children, two little ones.

ROBB: That wasn't very smart.

LEONA: My husband's not well.

ROBB: What's he got? Sperm depletion?

LEONA: Black lung. He can't raise no motherless children.

ROBB: Jesus, what is it with this place? Are you from here, Deemer?

DEEMER: Yes, sir.

ROBB: Don't they have anything better to do around here than die?

DEEMER: No, sir.

ROBB: You can't even ask somebody how they're doing without them telling you about their damn colon. (*To JANNIE.*) What the hell are we doing here? It's a damn death town. (*To DEEMER.*) Get up there and see what's happening.

CLAUDE: It's only the Rescue Squad.

DEEMER: Looks like they're trying to back up the ambulance over the bank parking lot. Uh-oh. They backed up over one of them bodies, looks like.

LEONA: And I got me my two youngest girls ain't even in school yet.

ROBB: They play with Barbie dolls?

LEONA: Not in my house! I won't have none of them things in my house.

DEEMER: Leona's tabernacle.

LEONA: Evil things.

ROBB: Barbie's got the stiffest damn tits.

LEONA: You can't tell me the devil don't have a hand in it, all them dolls and robots.

ROBB: I go home and the damn living room floor is covered with Barbie dolls. Everywhere. I mean, you step on a damn Barbie doll, and the tits will break your foot.

JANNIE: They're only dolls, Robb.

ROBB: Barbie's got her own office and her own sportscar and a swimming pool. Tell me what Ken's got. Go on. He dudden even have a dick. You ever looked between Ken's legs?

LEONA: I know what I'd do, and I'd do it, too.

ROBB: I bet you run a tight ship, Leona. My mom sure as hell did.

LEONA: I do what I can, with the Almighty Everlasting's help.

ROBB: I wish He'd help Jannie. Our house looks like a damn toy store hit by some tornado, and that's on a good day. Jannie is the only person I know who discusses cleaning the house with the damn vacuum cleaner. And then puts it on a list.

LEONA: I think I'll have me an RC.

ROBB: Help yourself. We've got Jannie's lists all over the house. She's got lists about the lists.

(LEONA gets herself an RC from the cooler, but she's smart enough to prop the door open.)

Big Claude, you see any Marines yet?

CLAUDE: No.

ROBB: Then we're OK. That's the only thing I'm afraid of. Marines shoot and ask questions later.

DEEMER: They're still working to get those bodies on the ambulance over at the bank.

ROBB: I'll tell you who it is. It's Shiftlet and that guy's always trying to sell me life insurance and one of the Filipino doctors, Guanzo, the one drives a Mercedes 560 SEL. Shit, did you see old fat Wanda fly? Up against the wall and melted like a frozen lardball. And the dog! Jesus. Pure stop action.

DEEMER: That was some dead-eye shootin, Coach. Me and
    Claude was watching it all.

ROBB: I had me some little help.

CLAUDE: Audie Murphy.

ROBB: "Audie Murphy World War II M1."

DEEMER: It sure done the job.

ROBB: He sure did.

DEEMER: What kind of scope you got on that thing, Coach?

ROBB: Scope? They don't put scopes on combat weaponry.
    Scopes are for psychopaths, deerhunters– That's the
    beauty of this *Gun of the Month* thing. You sign on, and
    they send you a gun every damn month of the year.
    Museum quality, limited edition, twelve historic guns
    that made this country work right. What could be wrong
    with that? Shit, they give you up to five months to pay.
    (*Pause.*) A gun for every occasion. Upstairs, here, "Audie
    Murphy". Downstairs– Downstairs seemed to require a
    more High Noon approach, a friendlier gun, like "The
    Duke", here. Next month "The Belle Starr Petite
    Derringer". The promo says it's not but four inches long,
    but damn thing works pretty as clockwork– (*To LEONA*.)
    Hey mama, get Jannie a Coke.

JANNIE: I don't want a Coke.

ROBB: It'll calm your stomach. You always say it does.

JANNIE: I'm fine.

ROBB: You look sick.

JANNIE: I'm fine.

ROBB: Just don't puke. It makes me sick when you puke.

DEEMER: You want some Tums, Mrs Lambert?

JANNIE: No

ROBB: I bet Claude likes guns.

DEEMER: He likes shooting pigeons up on the roof.

ROBB: Letting them fly up, then popping them off one by one.

JANNIE: Stop!

ROBB: What?

JANNIE: People are dead out there! They're dead!

ROBB: They're not dead.

DEEMER: They're pretty dead, Coach.

JANNIE: Wanda and Cooter and the Bread Man–

ROBB: They're not people.

DEEMER: Not Cooter, anyways.

ROBB: They're only pieces, Jannie. Tell them about the pigeons, Claude, how they start flying and your eye sees not something living but pieces moving, shapes or dark things against the light but definitely not alive. You've got your basic quick and your basic dead.

LEONA: Blasphemer.

ROBB: Oh, no, mom. That is one thing I am not. I have never blasphemed. Nothing percolates in my brain but truth.

LEONA: Somebody should of taught you a lesson a long time ago.

ROBB: You do it, momma. Go on. Here I am. Teach me. I'm waiting. Go on. I want you to teach me. Do it. (*Then.*) You missed your chance to save my soul.

(*ROBB and LEONA stare at each other. LEONA walks to front door and exits. ROBB kneels behind the bunker, takes aim with "The Duke".*)

JANNIE: No, Robb, no!

(*ROBB fires. Offstage in the street, LEONA screams and falls. ROBB ejects the cartridge and reloads.*)

JANNIE: Oh, my God!

ROBB: I never did like her.

DEEMER: Leona had her days.

ROBB: Today probably wasn't one of them. Unbelievable. Look at that hair. It never even moved.

(*ROBB hands "The Duke" to CLAUDE.*)

Now I can breathe. (*To CLAUDE.*) Keep an eye on things. (*Pause.*) So, Deemer. What do you think they'll do about the game tonight? Reschedule or forfeit? Twenty they forfeit. Twenty we would have beat their damn butts.

DEEMER: Even with Castlewood niggers?

ROBB: I've got a new play. It's a damn work of art. I can't even get it on the board, it's so damn mental. I had to conceive of it without words and then invent new words for it. It's like an attitude. I've waited my whole life for this play.

DEEMER: Defense or offense?

ROBB: Both at the same time.

DEEMER: Do you pass the ball or run it?

ROBB: You ride the ball.

DEEMER: You want another beer, Coach?

ROBB: I want a ball.

(*ROBB picks up a canned ham.*)

Great. OK. This is a football. But it's not a football.

DEEMER: It's a ham, looks like.

ROBB: What I'm holding in my hands is nothing but the end of a long piece of string, and all I've got to do is start winding it up, see, and winding, and if I concentrate on winding the string, and nothing else, what I'll end up with is what?

CLAUDE: A ball of string.

ROBB: Good!

DEEMER: A ball of string?

ROBB: That's how you score.

DEEMER: How?

ROBB: You let the ball carry you there. We're not the force. Get that out of your head. Get it out. We don't carry the ball. The ball carries you. All you've got to do is wind it up. Pick up that string.

DEEMER: And you put this string out on the field?

ROBB: The point's moot as shit but we would have won. The only trouble's counting on teenager brains. They can't take in the magnitude.

(*ROBB turns his back to JANNIE. He points to a white stripe running down his back.*)

Look at this.

JANNIE: What?

ROBB: I spent the night on the damn fifty yard line. Tell me that's not crazy. Balanced there, on the line. I could have fallen either way. But I had "The Duke", so I was ready, and then the whole play came to me, clear as a bell.

JANNIE: Robb. Is it me?

ROBB: You?

JANNIE: I did something.

(*ROBB laughs.*)

What?

ROBB: Did she do something? (*To DEEMER.*) Tell her, sport.

DEEMER: Me, Coach?

JANNIE: Robb, what?

ROBB: Big Claude knows. He knows all my secrets. He knew I was upstairs. We had a chat.

JANNIE: What did I do?

ROBB: Claude doesn't have to talk much because he's one of those secure kind of guys who knows his position in the universe. Everything has to have its own position. You can't have your boots all over your bib overalls, now. There may be an order. (*Pause.*) You tell me, Jannie. What exactly is your position in the universe?

JANNIE: I don't know, Robb.

ROBB: I didn't think so.

JANNIE: With you and the girls?

ROBB: Right! With me and the girls. Working on this premise, let's go over it very carefully. With me and the girls is not here in this joke store. Neither is it in Wish Campbell's pants.

JANNIE: Wish?

ROBB: I don't want to hear about it.

JANNIE: Wish Campbell?

ROBB: I don't want to hear about it.

DEEMER: The mortician?

ROBB: I'd say morticians do it like everybody else.
(*DEEMER and CLAUDE laugh.*)

Do they, Jannie? (*Pause.*) Jesus, Jannie, in our own house,
our own miserable little piece of shit house with all those
ceilings swirling around and those damn gold flecks in
the plaster.

JANNIE: Wish was picking up some sewing.

ROBB: Sewing.

JANNIE: I was making baby clothes for his wife.

ROBB: For money? (*Pause.*) I asked you a question!

JANNIE: Twelve dollars. Twelve whole dollars! Are you
satisfied.

ROBB: (*Calm.*) I asked you to quit sewing for people.

JANNIE: I did.

ROBB: It didn't look right. Sewing for people is like idiot
work.

JANNIE: Wish was picking up baby clothes, Robb, that's all.

ROBB: Did you sew the baby clothes?

JANNIE: Yes, but–

ROBB: Then you lied to me.

JANNIE: I didn't mean–

ROBB: She can sit up all night making some damn dress,
getting it perfect. She can do that. Why can't she do
anything else?

JANNIE: Robb. (*Pause.*) Is it because of my sewing?

ROBB: She'll sew all night, and some old lady pays her
fifteen dollars. It duddent make any sense. We're going
to vote. Jury, are you listening?

DEEMER: Who?

ROBB: You're the jury, you and Big Claude.

DEEMER: OK.

ROBB: I saw the way Wish Campbell was walking out of
my front door.

DEEMER: How, Coach?

ROBB: Big. Claude knows about those big walkers, don't you Big Claude? Wish was walking big.

(*CLAUDE laughs.*)

JANNIE: He had the baby clothes in his hand.

ROBB: You lied to me.

JANNIE: I didn't.

ROBB: You got out of position, Jannie. You veered.

JANNIE: Do you really think Wish and I would have been stupid enough to do something like that right there in the neighborhood?

ROBB: She doesn't like the neighborhood.

JANNIE: I didn't say that, Robb.

ROBB: Tacky people, tacky little houses. The children smell funny. Deemer, what does tacky mean?

DEEMER: Beats me, Coach.

ROBB: You know, Claude?

CLAUDE: Not very nice.

ROBB: Jury, you can take my word for it. It is not very nice.

JANNIE: It's you that doesn't like the neighborhood. It's you that complained.

ROBB: Gentlemen of the jury, we've got these swirled ceilings. The plaster is all swirled around in big designs, and the ceilings are real low. I'll tell you something, people who live in houses like ours get cancer. That's why everybody dies here. They've all got swirled ceilings.

(*ROBB kicks the dead body of FATHER.*)

Ask *him.*

(*ROBB lifts the jacket from FATHER's face.*)

Jesus Christ.

JANNIE: It was Father.

ROBB: Uh-oh, that's a big one. Kill a priest, go straight to Hell. Do not pass go. Jesus. (*Pause.*) Deemer! Get him out of here. You and Claude.

DEEMER: Where?

ROBB: Anywhere. It gives me the creeps.

DEEMER: How about the cooler, Coach?

ROBB: Just do it. And clean up the blood. I don't like it.

> (*CLAUDE and DEEMER put FATHER in the cooler.*
> *DEEMER holds the door open for CLAUDE.*)

I didn't know it was him. He had all that junk on.

He was a damn African weirdo. Nine thirty on a Monday night, our priest drops by. I'm in my damn skivvies watching Monday Night Football.

JANNIE: He was lonely.

ROBB: He belonged in church. Not at my house. He was this piece coming out of nowhere 9:30 on a Monday night ringing the damn doorbell. Deemer, who are we playing tonight?

DEEMER: Castlewood Vikings.

ROBB: Vikings.

DEEMER: Undefeated. All State two years in a row.

ROBB: Bloody Goths and Long John Silver. We'd of whipped their tails.

DEEMER: Our boys been playing some ball.

ROBB: Jannie hates football.

JANNIE: I don't.

ROBB: There it is. Jury, you heard it right there.

JANNIE: Robb, I don't.

ROBB: Jannie thinks it's a game. She thinks selling shoes is serious stuff or insurance or some jerk at IBM who can't even explain to his own mother what they pay him to do all day. I know what I do. I know exactly what I do. What I do is mathematical. Football is more mathematical than the math classes they pay me to teach, because football is one of the few useful models of a finite set in the universe.

> (*ROBB assembles a "football team" on the counter using beer bottles, the clock, boots, nab packages, whatever.*)

You've got your players and they run plays and you've got the ball and within the game you've got a certain number of variables, people's fuckups and things; but the beauty of it is that the whole thing is this knowable damn set, and that's my job. You work on your control, and you screw the boys' heads on tighter and tighter and they start to cook and the variables start dropping out and you stop getting the wildcards. What you is 11x (for play) equals G for game. You got it? OK. Now. Life, on the other hand is not a finite set.

You run your play and zap, this piece comes out of nowhere, out of the sky or out of the earth. The priest drops by 9:30 on a Monday night. The bank president's got a damn queer son so he won't give you a loan for a camper and the ceilings are swirling around with all this damn ugly plaster with gold flakes in it.

(*ROBB sweeps the "team" off the counter with his arm.*)

Life doesn't have any brackets, Jannie. I don't like that. It's just all these pieces flying out of nowhere. There aren't any time outs. There aren't any refs calling fouls.

(*A TROOPER lunges through front door wearing riot gear. He has a gun on CLAUDE, who is holding "The Duke".*)

TROOPER: Hold it right there! What the hell is going on, Claude? I ought to blow your fucking face off!

ROBB: I'm glad to see somebody's on the ball out there.

TROOPER: Coach! We didn't know you was in here. You all get the hell out of here.

ROBB: (*To CLAUDE.*) Give me "The Duke", Big Claude.

JANNIE: No, please!

TROOPER: Watch it, Coach. We don't need no more heroes today.

(*ROBB points "The Duke" at JANNIE's head.*)

ROBB: Everything's under control, just don't move a muscle.

TROOPER: What the–

ROBB: Take his gun, Claude. Trust me. I may have only one shot, and you may get me, but if anyone's going with me, it's her.

(*CLAUDE takes the gun from the TROOPER.*)

TROOPER: Listen, Claude–

ROBB: Do I know you?

TROOPER: You started my boy this year. Running back. (*Pause.*) We thought you was Claude, drunk.

ROBB: Is your boy the big one or the little one?

TROOPER: He's right big.

ROBB: The Big 'un. He's the only beef I had this season. You got yourself some college ball material.

TROOPER: Yeah?

ROBB: Get the flab off and keep his grades up and you'll hear those knocks on the front door, this spring.

TROOPER: You think so?

ROBB: Good chance of it.

TROOPER: We was hoping to see him at Tech.

ROBB: The point is to get him to the pros, so you and the Mrs can retire.

TROOPER: It'd be nice.

ROBB: I've got girls. Tallest damn girls you've ever seen.

TROOPER: Listen, Coach– we didden have no idea it was you in here doing all this– come on– let me walk you out of here–

ROBB: I wouldn't last one second out that door, and you know it.

TROOPER: Naw.

ROBB: They'll kill me.

TROOPER: No, sir. No way. Not after the kind of season you give our boys. We're gonna whip the pants off Castlewood tonight.

ROBB: I've worked out a new play. I need to get it to the boys.

TROOPER: No problem.

ROBB: Would they let me go to the game?

TROOPER: Sure.

ROBB: (*Laughs.*) You think I'm crazy?

TROOPER: You got the pressures of the game and all–

ROBB: I want my kids here. My girls.

JANNIE: The girls–

ROBB: You go back out there and tell your buddies I want to see my kids. When I see them, here, you'll get me.

JANNIE: No, Robb!

TROOPER: Coach, we got rules 'bout things like that.

JANNIE: He'll hurt them.

ROBB: I just want to see them. Sarah's at the elementary school, and Molly's at home with a sitter.

TROOPER: I don't know–

ROBB: Half an hour. I'll give you half an hour.

TROOPER: I'll do what I can, Coach. Why don't you let me take these folks with me? Go on and let them go.

ROBB: (*Pause.*) No.

TROOPER: You can keep Claude.

ROBB: I need them here. I need the company. Get out of here. And get some weight off your boy.

TROOPER: Listen, Coach, they got all kinds of doctors over to Castlewood for this kind of thing. They can help you, Coach, and you'd be back coaching 'fore you know it–

ROBB: Get my kids. And get some weight off your boy.

TROOPER: Think about it now, Coach. Give us the sign out there, and you'll walk. I'll be waiting.

(*Reluctantly, TROOPER exits.*)

ROBB: Who's got a watch? What's the time? Where the damn clock?

DEEMER: On the counter.

(*ROBB picks up the wall clock and checks it.*)

ROBB: All righty. We'll take a breather.

DEEMER: They thought you was Claude, and we thought you was Tottie Crabtree.

ROBB: Tottie Crabtree?

DEEMER: On account of him taking a shotgun into the bank last week looking for Mr Shiftlet 'cause Tottie didn't want to pay no more on his farm. Leona said it was because they gave away his Christmas Club money to his wife.

ROBB: Shiftlet comes to me. 'Lambert, give my boy a chance.' And his kid is queerer than all get out: dudden even have any damn pubic hair yet, and the old man's making him go out for football. They would of killed the boy out there, and Shiftlet thinks it'll make a man out of him. I sent the kid home, and that's why Shiftlet wouldn't give me the loan. See how it all comes together, how the pieces fit? All I did was put old Shiftlet out of his misery. Claude! You want me to put you out of your misery? They'll shut this place down, Claude, and you'll be out on the street. Nothing but the SSI check once a month. I'll be glad to save you. Give me the word.

DEEMER: That ain't funny, Coach.

ROBB: And who's hiring halfwit bag boys these days? Safeway's got damn PHDs bagging groceries.

DEEMER: They ain't shutting us down.

ROBB: This place is a joke.

JANNIE: Like my sewing is a joke.

ROBB: Look at this place! My wife runs a damn joke store. What are you all pretending today: that somebody's just dying to buy pig balls?

CLAUDE: One of the trooper cars is pulling out.

DEEMER: My cousin works down to the memory gardens says come this summer they'll need a new mower man 'round the grave stones and I'm good with a mower, I told him.

ROBB: Don't worry. I'll make this place famous. You can sell souvenirs, little statuettes of Shiftlet and Guanzo and we've got to have one of that old dog.

DEEMER: Cooter.

JANNIE: Why didn't you shoot me? When I was in the street looking up at you, why didn't you shoot?

ROBB: Why didn't you run? (*Pause.*) You had it.

JANNIE: I don't know.

ROBB: It wasn't in the game plan. You have to stay in until the time runs out. No subs this quarter, babe.

JANNIE: I won't let the girls in here. If I see them, if they bring them here, I don't care, I'll run.

ROBB: What about Deemer and Claude?

JANNIE: We'll all three run.

ROBB: You would do that for them, wouldn't you?

JANNIE: They aren't bringing the girls in here.

ROBB: Would you do it for me?

JANNIE: (*Pause.*) What?

ROBB: Save me.

JANNIE: I tried.

ROBB: Nuh-uh.

JANNIE: I did. I would of done anything, Robb.

ROBB: You didn't.

JANNIE: Please...

ROBB: I was shit to you. I was hell to you.

JANNIE: You weren't.

ROBB: Because you loved me.

JANNIE: More than anything.

ROBB: Some people get things confused. They can't keep things clear in their head about what is what and what isn't. Like they think love is some kind of answer, and it isn't no such thing, babe. Love's just another damn variable. Go out for a pass, Big Claude.

(*ROBB passes the ham football to CLAUDE who catches it neatly.*)

We got us a lineman with hands, a damn bluechipper guard. Claude, here, tells me he was all-state guard–

DEEMER: Two years in a row.

ROBB: (*To CLAUDE.*) That kind of personal excellence will take you far in life, Big Claude. Here!

(*CLAUDE passes football ham back to ROBB.*)

DEEMER: Here, Coach!

ROBB: Don't tell me you were a bluechipper, too, Deemer–

DEEMER: No, sir.

ROBB: All-state–

(*ROBB passes football ham to DEEMER.*)

DEEMER: You OK, Coach?

ROBB: It's my damn back. Jesus. (*To JANNIE.*) Fix it. Come on, Jannie. Fix it for me.

(*ROBB hands "The Duke" to CLAUDE, sweeps everything off the counter to the floor, then climbs onto the check out counter. He stretches out on his stomach. Slowly, JANNIE goes to him. She reaches out, then puts her hands on his skin and holds them there as if trying to transmit something to him or to take something away. JANNIE starts to rub ROBB's back.*)

That's great. God, that's good. You're the only one who knows where the pain is.

JANNIE: I wish you would see somebody.

ROBB: And let some chink knife me for a thousand bucks?

JANNIE: They're not chinks.

ROBB: Hell, I'm lucky it's only one vertebrae and not my knees or my shoulders.

DEEMER: You play pro ball, Coach?

ROBB: Sure thing, Deemer. Nine years with the Dallas Cowboys.

DEEMER: You mean it?

JANNIE: He was a junior college All-American.

ROBB: I make it look easy, don't I? Every Friday night.

DEEMER: I'd say it's right hard, Coach.

ROBB: Every damn game I die. Did you know that?

JANNIE: I know.

ROBB: But, I'm good.

DEEMER: Yes, sir.

ROBB: Yes, sir, what?

DEEMER: Yes, sir, Coach.

ROBB: Now you tell me if I'm so damn good, why can't I buy a camper? Every game I die, and my players– kids, rednecks– they drive better cars than I do. Explain that to me. Your folks sending the girls new clothes all the time–

JANNIE: They want to do it.

ROBB: Damn it. I'm their father. Don't you think I want to do it. I can't afford a damn camper. Wish Campbell's got a camper.

DEEMER: It's more like a RV, Coach. It's got a microwave oven in it, and a TV dish on top.

ROBB: Shiftlet and his damn fruit son.

JANNIE: That's not why he didn't give you the loan. All he had to do was look up our statements. It wasn't his son, Robb.

ROBB: Hey–

JANNIE: It was you joining *The Gun of the Month Club.*

ROBB: The guns are an investment. I told you–

JANNIE: We don't have anything to invest–

ROBB: You buy your kids a color TV they want a VCR or some kind of tennis shoes with names on'm. You can't get it figured out. You can't get the grass to grow in your backyard. You can't figure out how people buy furniture for their living room. You can't figure out why nothing's enough.

JANNIE: We would of had the money.

ROBB: What money?

JANNIE: If we hadn't moved...

ROBB: It's not the money. It's figuring things out.

JANNIE: We were Bears and Beavers and Tigers and Bobcats and Bulldogs and Squirrels–

ROBB: We weren't ever Squirrels–

JANNIE: All those times we moved, every new place we went to, I did for you. I never asked why. I'd pack up the trophies and the guns and unpack them and pack them back up–

ROBB: There was always another team waiting for me to fix it. Move in on it, put in on, bathe in it, and eat it, and think it, and sleep it and make it work.

JANNIE: You can't fix everything there is. Life's not football.

ROBB: Mine is.

JANNIE: I'm not football. The girls aren't football.

ROBB: Football kept me on this damn planet, Jannie. Football kept me in a clean position.

JANNIE: You had this one thing you controlled–

ROBB: Damn right I controlled it. Winning makes me breathe.

JANNIE: No–

ROBB: I am a missionary of football, and when it's rolling, damn it, I touch the Almighty, babe–

JANNIE: Then what's that? Out there?

ROBB: What?

JANNIE: Out there!

ROBB: That's my new play.

JANNIE: And that's going to fix everything? Me and the girls and everything–

ROBB: I've got the ball, and all I've got to do is wind it home. Nothing can stop me now.

JANNIE: (*Pause.*) You're crazy.

(*ROBB hits JANNIE across the face. She staggers back but doesn't cry.*)

ROBB: (*Pause.*) This is new. I've never hit you. What does it mean? Say something. Damn it!

JANNIE: I've been paying down on a camper at the Chevrolet place. It's used but they've cleaned it all up. It's in good shape. It's only got ten thousand miles.

ROBB: It's not going to be all right! Do you hear me! Nothing's going to be all right.

JANNIE: It's metallic blue with a white camper top and I can almost stand up in the back and it's got four beds–

ROBB: Look at me.

JANNIE: They're going to put in new carpet for me–

ROBB: Look at me!

JANNIE: (*Finally sobbing.*) I can't.

ROBB: Now we're getting somewhere.

JANNIE: (*Crying.*) On the back it's got painted "OFF TO SEE THE WIZARD" with quotation marks around it, and I thought we could paint our names on, too. "OFF TO SEE THE WIZARD" (*Pause.*) Robb, Jannie, Sarah and Molly.

ROBB: Gentlemen of the jury, we have made a major breakthrough today. My wife has begun to know the truth. The scales have fallen from her eyes.

JANNIE: That's why I took this job. That's why I worked in a joke store. You wouldn't let me sew–

ROBB: You're fixed, babe. I fixed you. Aren't you going to thank me?

JANNIE: Thank you.

ROBB: Your eyes were like fish eyeballs staring at me. Tell us about fish eyeballs, Claude.

CLAUDE: They don't blink.

ROBB: Never damn do. Just keep staring like a damn statue of the Virgin Mary. There's nothing to see, Jannie.

JANNIE: You're not going to hurt the girls.

ROBB: Shit. What time is it?

(*ROBB picks up the clock from the counter and checks the time.*) The damn thing's not working!

DEEMER: It probably needed a little gravity to pull the hands around, but Mrs Lambert wanted us to take it down and fix it.

JANNIE: It was eight minutes slow.

ROBB: You are death. Do you realise that? Everything you touch dies. What's the fucking time? Look at the bank clock.

DEEMER: You shot it out.

(*ROBB crosses to JANNIE and puts the gun to her head.*)

CLAUDE: The trooper car is back.

DEEMER: Hey, Coach, it sure is. Looks like they got your little girls, too.

ROBB: Nuh-uh. You sure they're not midget cops in drag?

DEEMER: You see them little hairbraids, Claude?

(*ROBB looks out the front door.*)

ROBB: They brought the damn sitter.

JANNIE: They couldn't have.

ROBB: They did. Look.

JANNIE: They wouldn't do it. It's a trap.

ROBB: They brought the damn sitter. God what jokers.

JANNIE: It's a trap, Robb.

DEEMER: They're putting the girls behind this big shield thing.

ROBB: Where?

DEEMER: Over behind the funeral parlor. See them troopers bending over talking to them.

ROBB: Claude?

CLAUDE: I don't see them.

DEEMER: Look, there.

ROBB: I can't believe this.

JANNIE: (*Pause.*) You're sobering up.

ROBB: I need to be clear for this. I need to be clear.

JANNIE: You'll never do it sober.

ROBB: Do you think I didn't plan this? I knew Shiftlet would be in the bank parking lot at 9 am on the dot. There isn't any chance or random when you wind the ball. Everything makes sense. (*To DEEMER.*) Now what?

DEEMER: Nothing yet.

(*ROBB pushes CLAUDE away from door.*)

ROBB: What the hell are they doing? What's the hold-up?

(*Yelling out the door.*) Come on! Time's running out! I want the girls!

(*Pause.*) Deemer, get your tail over there. Tell them I want the girls here now.

DEEMER: Sure, Coach.

(*DEEMER exits from front door, running.*)

JANNIE: They're buying time.

ROBB: Shut up.

JANNIE: They're going to kill you.

ROBB: They'll have to get past you to do it.

JANNIE: Deemer's free. (*Getting stronger.*) Now it's just me and Claude. They'll sacrifice us.

ROBB: Your eyes are different.

JANNIE: They'll blow this place up if they have to.

ROBB: (*Pause.*) You've stopped. I thought saints never stopped. (*Pause.*) Look, do me a favor. Just make sure they know it wasn't football. They're good boys.

JANNIE: You can tell them.

ROBB: I don't think so. Tell them anything. Tell them it was the ceilings swirling around. (*Pause.*) They won't believe you, though. Be sure and tell them about my new play. The new coach may want to try it.

JANNIE: Claude and I can walk you out. You could walk between us.

ROBB: (*Laughs.*) You can't stop. Look what I do for you and the love keeps pouring out. Well, we're even. I can't stop winding the ball. What do you think, Big Claude?

CLAUDE: I don't blame God.

ROBB: Me neither.

CLAUDE: Dinosaurs lived on this planet for seventy-five million years.

ROBB: Jesus. Seventy-five million years and then nothing.

CLAUDE: But I don't blame God.

ROBB: God keeps his nose out of it. You can't tell me he doesn't see all those shopping malls and swimming pools and gets disgusted, but he keeps his nose out of it. Get us a beer, Big Claude.

(*CLAUDE starts to cross to the cooler.*)

I'll get it. You keep your eye on those old boys out there. I don't trust them. And let me know if you see the girls.

(*ROBB props open the cooler door.*)

(*To JANNIE.*) You get up the ladder.

(*ROBB backs into cooler. "The Duke" is pointed at JANNIE until it disappears into the cooler. We hear ROBB stumble, fall, and the gun drops.*)

I tripped over a damn dead priest. Where are the lights in here?

JANNIE: Over by the door.

(*JANNIE climbs down ladder and crosses to cooler to help ROBB.*)

It's a chain hanging down and you pull.

ROBB: He's so damn black I didn't see him.

(*Suddenly, electrified, JANNIE pushes the cooler door shut. ROBB struggles from inside the cooler.*)

JANNIE: Help me, Claude! Oh, please God, help me, Claude, please!

(*CLAUDE watches calmly, then crosses to cooler door. He pushes and the door catches and locks shuts. CLAUDE gets his dolly and begins taking bunker apart, he loads the bags into the elevator.*)

ROBB: (*From inside cooler.*) Jannie! Open the door, Jannie.
(*Calmly.*) They'll kill me Jannie. Open the door.

(*ROBB knocks on the cooler door to get out.*)

(*Pause.*) Are you there? Jannie? Jannie!

(*JANNIE stretches herself across the cooler door as if making final contact with ROBB, as if reaching through it.*)

JANNIE: I'm here. (*Pause.*) We'll move again. We'll have the camper, and we'll move. The camper's blue. It's only got ten thousand miles. It really looks almost new. They said it was this old couple that owned it, and then the husband died and his wife didn't want it any more. (*Pause.*) We'll move some place where we can go camping, some place with a lot of parks. We'll look at the map, and we'll choose a good place, maybe near the beach. We'll get away from the mountains, Robb, we'll move. You can get a job any place you want, and we'll move again. and we won't live in a house with swirled ceilings, I promise. And I won't sew, and I won't work because we'll already have the camper.

ROBB: (*From inside cooler.*) Jannie– We're here.

(*Inside the cooler there is a gunshot. JANNIE flinches then staggers backward until she hits the counter, stepping on her purse. She turns to see her things splashed across the floor where ROBB threw them. JANNIE stoops and collects one by one the papers, book keeping books, her purse and lunch bag. DEEMER enters.*)

DEEMER: Where's Coach? They almost got them bodies up, but there's a bunch of blood still places though. You know that weather girl from over to Channel 6, one wears the hats from TV and the teeth? She's over to the funeral home with a bunch of movie cameras and lights and things and she talked to me about what'd been happening in here and all and she said I'd be on TV tonight and you can be, too, Claude, you come on. See if Coach'll let you come on.

(*DEEMER exits out front door. JANNIE clutches her things tight to her chest with her left hand. In her right is a checkbook.*)

JANNIE: The checkbook was here all the time. I knew it was–

(*JANNIE is transfigured. She exits out the front door, leaving CLAUDE all alone. CLAUDE stands against the cooler door, listening and knocking. Blackout. Curtain. Amen.*)